Crazy Quilt Patchwork

A Quick and Easy Approach with 19 Projects

Dixie Haywood

DOVER PUBLICATIONS, INC.
NEW YORK

Published in Canada by General Publishing Company, Ltd., 30 Lesmill Road,
Don Mills, Toronto, Ontario.
Published in the United Kingdom by Constable and Company, Ltd.

This Dover edition, first published in 1986, is a corrected and slightly abridged
republication of *Crazy Quilting with a Difference*, first published by Scissortail
Publications, Pensacola, Florida in 1981. Of the eight color pages in the original
edition, seven have been omitted and one appears in black and white on page 30.

Manufactured in the United States of America
Dover Publications, Inc., 31 East 2nd Street, Mineola, N.Y. 11501

Library of Congress Cataloging-in-Publication Data

Haywood, Dixie.
    Crazy quilt patchwork.

    Rev. ed. of: Crazy quilting with a difference. 1981.
    Bibliography: p.
    Includes index.
    1. Quilting. 2. Patchwork. I. Haywood, Dixie. Crazy quilting with a dif-
ference. II. Title.
TT835.H353   1986   746.46   85-25320
    ISBN 0-486-25042-3 (pbk.)

CONTENTS

Dedicated To

All whose generosity of spirit makes quilting a joy,
especially
Joan Hart, Carter Houck, Pat Cox, Pat Morris and Mike Wigg.

Preface

My first book, THE CONTEMPORARY CRAZY QUILT PROJECT BOOK, introduced the technique for making crazy quilting into an actual quilting method. I have continued to explore the possibilities of contemporary crazy quilting; this book is the result. I hope CRAZY QUILT PATCHWORK will make it easier for beginners to get started, while introducing exciting new dimensions to those already intrigued by the possibilities of designing in the cloth.

In addition to those mentioned in the text, I am grateful for the help from Priscilla Miller of Concord Fabrics, Inc., who provided much of the fabric used in the projects; and to Donna Wilder and Anita Wellings of Fairfield Processing Corporation, who furnished the batting. Many fellow authors answered questions and shared information that was truly valuable. Their help is especially appreciated.

My husband, Bob, deserves special thanks for the photography, proofreading, back rubs, and preventing the premises from being condemned by the Health Department.

Chapter One

Not So Crazy Quilting

When crazy quilting is mentioned, most people think of the elaborate concoctions of the Victorians. With the Victorian crazy quilt, the use of fancy fabric and fancier embellishment reached heights of luxury and lunacy. A well done Victorian crazy quilt is an extravagant joy; a bad one could be loved only by its maker.

Victorian crazy quilting did not spring into existence spontaneously, but grew from the scrap quilts of less affluent times. When warmth was needed quickly and materials were scarce, random scraps were pieced together without wasted time or fabric. Very few of these early crazy quilts remain, a fact that testifies to their function as utility bedcoverings. Significantly, you could almost cover the country with extant Victorian crazy quilts. Whether magnificent or mediocre, they were essentially useless.

Contemporary crazy quilting is really not-so-crazy quilting; it combines the fun of the Victorian crazy quilt with the utility of earlier versions. Two quilting traditions are involved. The Victorian quilt contributes the possibilities for a play of line and color, enhanced by embroidery. The utilitarian string quilt offers the press method of piecing that makes it possible to piece on the sewing machine without stitching being visible. It allows freedom to use embroidery for emphasis, rather than as the means of construction.

Contemporary crazy quilting differs from the Victorian crazy quilt in the basic approaches to quilting, piecing and stitchery. It is a rare Victorian crazy quilt that is quilted. Most of them had no batting at all. When it was used, the batting was fastened in place after the top was constructed. With contemporary crazy quilting the fabric is quilted through batting as it is pieced, adding both warmth and texture.

Traditionally, the fabric for a crazy quilt was either taken as it was found in the scrap, or cut to shape before it was embroidered in place. With spectacular exceptions, the shape of the fabric was not as important as the embroidery that held it. The Victorian crazy quilt was more often a display of needle skills than of design ability.

Fabric shapes are of primary concern in contemporary crazy quilting. The fabric is pieced with a "design as you go" technique. Except for the first piece used, the fabric is not cut until it has been sewn in place and can be seen in relation to the previous piecing. Initially this can be unnerving to those used to graphing out a pattern in advance, but with a little practice it is great fun to design in the cloth. In Chapter Two you will find a series of piecing suggestions to help you get started.

The option to use as much or as little stitchery as desired, or even none at all, is an often overlooked feature of contemporary crazy quilting. Since stitchery is not essential to the construction, it can be used to emphasize a line and enhance the overall design. This is a case where "less is more"; a little stitchery judiciously applied can have more of an impact than random excesses with needle and thread.

NOT SO CRAZY QUILTING

The basis for the process is the "blank", which is constructed of a backing and batting. The backing fabric varies, depending on the project, from batiste to heavy Pellon.* Pellon is very useful in handbags, book covers and other projects where firmness is desired. Do not use a bias Pellon; it will not provide the stability needed. A batiste weight fabric is good for blanks that will be used in clothing when texture without bulk is needed. For the majority of projects, a muslin weight is ideal.

I've been experimenting with the use of a paper backing that is removed after the piecing is complete, a method used generations ago. Because it eliminates the extra layer of fabric, it is especially useful in clothing or where you wish to hand quilt. A new product called Stitch-n-Tear gives the same effect as paper but has advantages that paper lacks. It removes easily, but is more flexible than paper to work with and does not tear as readily when you are sewing.

The back of the blank will be covered when the project is completed, so any fabric of the desired weight can be used. This is a way to use up fabric that you wonder why you ever bought! Preshrink, of course. Don't overlook used fabric. Sheets are great, but check that they take a needle well or you may think you're embroidering through canvas.

Batting can be varied depending on the project and the fabric being used in the backing and piecing. I generally use a thick polyester bonded batting because I like the texture that results and it is easy to handle. Needlepunch or lightweight polyester batting is especially good for clothing where less bulk is desired, or when using very lightweight fabrics. Since the backing fabric and batting are stitched together and treated as one piece, more than one layer of batting can be used in a blank. The batting does not need to be in one piece. Batting scraps can be used by butting the edges together when constructing the blank. The batting will be secured by the quilting.

Five different fabrics are a good number with which to start, although I have used as few as three and as many as ten. I don't recommend this to beginners because of the balancing problems that arise with either too few or too many fabrics. I usually use a mix of prints and solids. Combinations of solids can be effective, but an all print selection is difficult. Embroidery may not show on print fabric and the overall effect is, to my taste at least, too chaotic. If the fabric you are using is yardage rather than scraps, cut it to eight to ten inch widths for easier handling. Preshrink the fabric and press it before starting to crazy quilt. Pressing afterwards should be done lightly or not at all, since it will flatten the batting.

Crazy quilting is a good way to empty your bobbins and use up odd color thread. The top thread will not show unless sheer fabric is used and the bobbin thread will be covered when the project is completed.

This is one form of patchwork where the grain of the fabric is usually unimportant because the blank acts as a stabilizer. Fabric can be sewn and cut without regard to the straight of grain unless the pattern of the fabric is being used to achieve a specific effect.

There may be a little reduction in size caused by the quilting. It varies according to the size of the blank, the scale of the piecing, the fabric being used and the thickness of the batting. I adjust for it with larger blanks and in closely fitted clothing. The directions for the project will indicate where to take this reduction into consideration; otherwise it should not be a problem. Occasionally distortion will occur and the completed piece will be slightly skewed. This is not serious; the distortion usually is corrected by construction of the project.

*Pellon is the name of a brand of nonwoven interfacing. Any similar interfacing may be used.

To construct the blank, cut the backing fabric and batting to the desired shape. Machine baste them together with the backing fabric on top, using the longest stitch on your sewing machine. (Don't worry that the batting will catch in the feed dogs; it won't.) In some projects, batting in the seam allowance adds undesirable bulk in the finished project. In such cases, make a specific seam allowance on the blank (usually 1/4") and trim the batting from the seam allowance before starting to crazy quilt. If the batting is not to be trimmed, machine baste without regard to the seam allowance.

Turn the batting side up. Cut the first piece of fabric to the shape you want. (This is the only piece you should cut in advance.) Pin it to the blank; do not sew it in place. You can start any place on the blank, but once you start, always work outward from the fabric. Don't start piecing in one place on the batting and then skip to another.

Lay the next fabric, uncut, right side down with the edges together. Check to be sure you will not sew over the pin holding the first piece in place; a pleat may form if you do. There is no need to pin the top piece. Machine stitch through the entire blank. Use about 1/4" seam allowance, being sure to catch the fabric underneath securely.

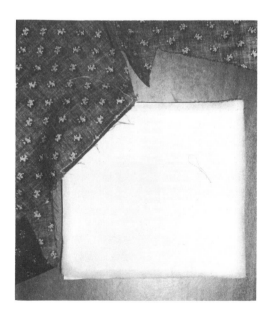

Open the fabric to the right side and cut it to the shape you want. Move the pin to this second piece. This will prevent it from moving and forming a bubble as the next piece is sewn.

Continue adding pieces by sewing uncut fabric in place, opening and cutting. If a light colored fabric is sewn over a darker one, be sure that you either cover the dark seam allowance fully with the lighter fabric or trim out the excess after the seam is sewn so the dark fabric will not show through. (If you discover you have neglected to do this after the piece is finished, don't despair. Plan your stitchery to hide it!)

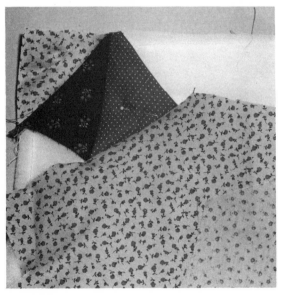

A common problem beginners seem to have is the formation of an inside angle. Inside angles are formed when the fabric extends beyond the edge of the previous piecing. There are several solutions: The inside angle can be covered with a convex curve; the next piece can be sewn across the angle; or one side of the next piece can be machine sewn and one side hand sewn.

A much better solution is not to form the inside angle in the first place. The problems in the preceeding picture are eliminated by cutting either EVEN WITH or BACK FROM the lines formed by the previous piecing. The left side was cut *even with* the line on the left. The right side was cut *back from* the line on the right.

An inside angle is also formed when a piece is sewn only part way along the edge of the previous fabric (the "line"). As piecing progresses, lines often become long. This seems to concern people and they try to break up the lines with shorter pieces, thereby forming an inside angle.

The solution is to ALWAYS sew along the entire line (but not beyond it, which then causes the inside angle in the previous example). Do this even if you feel a line is getting too long. Then shorten the line by cutting so that the new piece forms two or more edges. Putting in small pieces against a long line only complicates the piecing and does nothing to advance the design, since the small pieces are usually far out of proportion to the preceding ones. Lines can also be shortened with the use of curves, examples of which will be shown in the next chapter.

Some pieces cannot be added by machine. Curves, with the seam allowance turned under, are pinned in place until the blank is completed. The curve edge is secured with embroidery after the piecing is finished. Curves are discussed in detail in Chapter Two.

As you proceed there will be several possible lines where you can add the next piece. A general rule is to piece on the longer line first. Working from this line will eventually extend a shorter line and make the piecing more balanced. If you add to the short line first, you will extend the longer line even further, making the short piece vastly out of proportion.

Continue piecing until the entire blank is covered. Turn it over and straight stitch or zig-zag along the edge of the blank so that the stitching will hold the edges in place without showing in the seams of your project. You probably have extended some of the fabric beyond the blank, so trim it back to the edge.

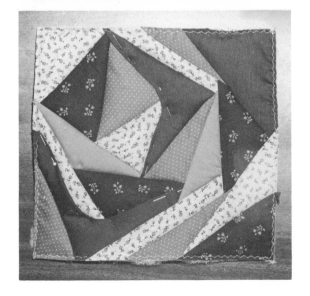

Now you have the basics of crazy quilting with a difference! Your piece is ready to embellish or not, as you wish.

Chapter Two

Piece By Piece

Now the fun begins! Once you understand the basic technique and the method for avoiding inside angles, you are ready to play with the possibilities of designing in the cloth. One of the exciting aspects of contemporary crazy quilting is the potential for individual expression. The examples and suggestions for fabric arrangements in this chapter are not for the purpose of creating a crazy-quilt-by-the-numbers formula (heaven forbid!) but to give an indication of the variety of approaches that can be used.

It seems a contradiction to show piecing arrangements while urging you not to plan too far ahead, but the contradiction is more apparent than real. Although some of the work in this book may look structured, I begin with only a general idea of the direction I want to take and usually just plan a piece or two in advance. Let the fabric tell you what to do. If you start with five or six fabrics in a mixture of prints and solids that have some relationship to each other, balance of color and shape will not be difficult. The shape of the blank you are working with will also be a factor. The crazy quilted bars in the Ice Ray quilt dictated a very linear piecing pattern, for example. The small triangular blanks and the fabrics — velvets, eyelet and calico prints — used in the Victoriana quilt led to smaller, more elaborate piecing. Conversely, a large blank will look better with larger piecing.

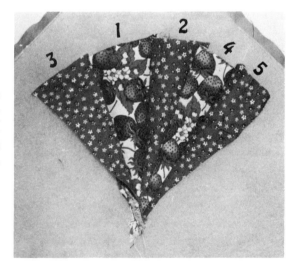

The majority of Victorian crazy quilts have shapes with no special system to their arrangement. When a design motif is used, I think it safe to say that the fan is the most popular. Fan piecing is probably the easiest to understand, so let's start with that.

A logical cap for a fan is a curve. Don't cut a curve to form one; cut a right angle or use a piece of fabric that has a right angle from a previous cut. This results in a much better curve. If you start with a curved cut, after clipping and turning under the seam allowance, you will end with a less interesting curve that often is too shallow for the area you want to cover. I discovered the best way to form a curve when I picked up a piece of fabric with a right angle cut into it. Rather than cutting out a curve, I just clipped the angle, turned under a seam allowance and laid it in place. That's what I mean by letting the fabric tell you what to do!

Curves also can be done in reverse. The previous example was a curve laid over piecing. The curve can be cut from fabric sewn in place, pulled back out of the way while the next piece is put underneath and then laid over and pinned in place. More than one fabric can be pieced under a curve, of course. This is especially effective with larger curves.

It is easier to piece a fan under a curve if the narrow ends of the fan point away from the curve, since it is difficult to control exactly where the points will meet. It can be done either way, however, giving you the control to achieve a special effect.

You should take advantage of the fact that curves can go in any direction. If all the curves are laid over previous piecing, they will march across your blank like geese following the leader. This can be effective occasionally; if it's all you do, it will be boring. A piecing arrangement I call an egg uses curves going in both directions. In its simple form, it is just two curves around a diamond. It can be more fun if you add variety to the center.

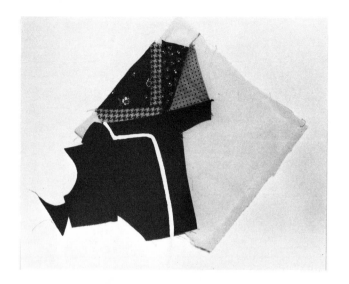

A double curve is a way to take advantage of a long line. It is, in fact, more effective done from a longer line than a shorter one. Be sure to leave the throat between double curves wide enough to turn under the seam allowance and still have room for embroidery. When first making a double curve, you might be more secure drawing the cutting lines on the fabric with a marking pen or a piece of chalk. After you've done a few, you'll find you can eyeball the cuts.

There is no need to cut fabric for each side of a double curve unless the curve is cut from such light fabric that the bottom fabric would show through. Place a single piece of fabric under the curves and pin in place. Cut the fabric even with or back from the lines and proceed with the piecing.

Triple curves are another possibility. This only looks complicated. Form a curve and pin in place over the previous piecing. Then cut double curves, arranging the throat between the second and third curves to fall approximately at the high point of the first curve. Lay fabric under the second and third curves, clip and turn under the seam allowance on the curves, and pin in place. Because of the angles involved, you usually will have to cut separate pieces to fit under the second and third curves.

14

There are two potential problems when piecing under curves. Be sure to place the pieces so the ends will be covered when you lay the curve in place. If you fail to plan for turning under the seam allowance of the curve, you'll see a batting gap. Should this happen, your alternatives are to take out the piecing and start over, or to add another piece of fabric. You might even want to do this on purpose!

The other potential problem is to extend the fabric or fabrics beyond the line of the curve, thereby forming an inside angle. It's helpful for beginners to draw lines on the batting as a boundary for the piecing.

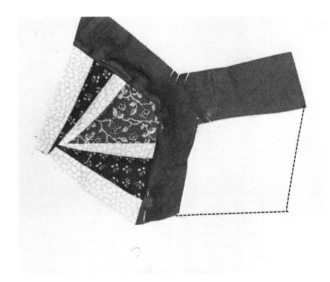

PIECE BY PIECE

It is no accident that the curve examples I have given are all concave curves. Although it is possible to use convex curves, I rarely do. The seam allowance is difficult to turn smoothly; even with careful clipping and trimming it has added bulk that gives a piled-on look. A convex curve can be helpful to fill an inside angle if you should blunder into one, but otherwise it does nothing that a concave curve can't do better.

It is not necessary to use curves to achieve a curved effect. Triangles can be used either alone or in conjunction with curves to create a spiral or to extend a line to a length that would be clumsy with a single curve. This is also useful when you want the movement that curves give without using embroidery, when you are using a print on which embroidery would not show well, or when you want to embroider through a general area of color instead of outlining the edges. Examples of using triangles in this way can be seen on both basket lids and on the stool cushion.

Curves and longer lines give crazy quilting a flow and movement that cannot be achieved with uniform sized pieces. By now I hope you have become convinced that a long line is an opportunity for interesting design rather than something about which to worry. Avoiding long lines is impossible; the nature of piecing makes them inevitable. Learn to use them to advantage.

In addition to letting the fabric tell you what to do, trust your own instincts. This is one type of quilting where there are no rules, only guidelines. No one can say that a piece of crazy quilting is wrong. It is true that some arrangements are better than others, but if it pleases you, it's right.

And if it doesn't please you, do another. Even if you are driven up the wall putting the first block together, do another. You'll find that you learned a lot doing the first and are beginning to enjoy yourself. With some things, repetition means boredom. Since no two pieces of crazy quilting are the same, repetition means learning and that leads to improvement. And fun.

Chapter Three

Focus On Design

Now that you have an idea of some piecing possibilities, how do you use them to design in the cloth with some sense of coherence? In addition to practice, experimentation helps. So does the concept of focus. While it might be a tour de force to combine all the piecing elements in Chapter Two in the same blank, I think you would be happier to selectively choose ideas from them to create a focal point. Let me reiterate that this does not mean to plan your piece in advance. If you want to do that, draft a pattern and make templates. The result may be terrific, but it won't be crazy quilting.

Starting in the center of a blank is an effective way to give some focus, especially if you do the major piecing in the center. Since you will be building out on all sides, the subsequent piecing acts as a frame for the center.

Starting in the center works especially well on a large blank because it allows the size of the pieces to be in better proportion. If you start at the edge of a large piece, the lines lengthen as the piecing proceeds. Even when you break them down effectively, there is a noticeable difference in proportion as you proceed. Sometimes this can be used to advantage, but it is more often a problem.

Always keep in mind how the blank will fit in the entire project. Sometimes the center of the blank will not be the focal point of the finished project. Be careful about starting in the center if the project you are making folds. Even if you don't start in the center, mark on the blank where the fold occurs so that you don't lose some special piecing when it is folded to either side.

You can help create focus by using long narrow strips as framing lines that lead the eye where you want emphasis. I find them useful not only to frame, but also as a transition between areas and as a secondary motif. Look for examples in the book cover, stool cushion, basket top and pillow, as well as in the Ice Ray quilt. It is better to sew on the straight grain when you will be cutting narrow strips. A bias strip often stretches and puckers as the next piece is sewn in place. Pin the strip with care so that only the tip of the pin is sewn over as the next piece is added. This usually will hold the strip in place without pleats being formed.

The colors that you use will, of course, help you focus the design. Whether you're picking colors from a color wheel or from instinct, you'll need lights, mediums and darks in a mixture of print sizes and solids. Even if you're using all solids, the combination of light, medium and dark shades is a basic concept. If you are having a problem finding enough fabrics that blend — less a problem now than a few years ago — don't overlook the possibility of using both the right and wrong sides of the same fabric.

Placement of the fabric within the crazy quilting does a lot to bring focus to a blank. If you look through the projects, you'll notice that I almost always use the same fabric under a double curve, and often under a triple curve. Fans are a natural for focus, but piecing them with a repeating color, either as a fan blade or as a strip between blades, gives even more emphasis. Enveloping curves become more important when they are tied together by the fabric used, whether as close in proximity as those in the egg arrangement or around larger areas of piecing.

Stitchery can be a major factor in achieving focus with your crazy quilting. You can subtly highlight fans, for instance, by working a chain stitch in each seam. When I use double or triple curves, I always embroider the same stitch on all edges of the curves for emphasis. The same thing can be done to connect areas on either side of a block that otherwise would not be seen as having a relationship.

As you piece, try to keep in mind the stitchery that may be used, especially on curves. For instance, a gold print may look just right under a brown curve but perhaps a brown print would be more effective than the gold one. Then gold embroidery could be used to close and accent the curve.

The Crazy Stars quilt is an attempt to use a motif while retaining a crazy quilting approach. I started with the idea of achieving a star-like block, but beyond that the blocks were not planned in advance. This kind of challenge is great fun; give it a try. Keep in mind, however, that balance and focus can be overdone. Don't make your piecing, color arrangement or stitchery too predictable. Crazy quilting implies a bit of spice and surprise!

Chapter Four

Quilting That Shows

The quilting in contemporary crazy quilting, in addition to providing warmth, gives depth and texture to the fabric. The esthetic qualities added by the quilting attract as much interest as the fact that it is quickly and easily done. In fact, since the stitches in the crazy quilting do not show in the finished piece, people sometimes do not understand that it *is* quickly and easily done!

I like the combination of solid color areas with crazy quilting, both to rest the eye and to emphasize the pieced sections. I enjoy hand quilting, so it was inevitable that I would combine crazy quilted blocks, where the quilting is apparent only in the resulting texture, with quilting that shows. Adding visible quilting is also functional, making it possible to use larger sections of solid color and giving a wider range of possible quilt sets. In addition, it can help to carry out the theme of a quilt, such as in the Crazy Stars or Crazy Amish quilts.

Designs for quilting can come from everywhere. The quilting in the Ice Ray quilt, which appears to be based on crazy quilting, is adapted from a design by that name for Chinese latticework. The Crazy Amish quilting designs are from traditional sources. The feathered plume in that quilt was worked out to fit the area using a template designed by Jean DuBois. Patricia Cox designed the quilted star especially for the Crazy Stars quilt, and has included it in a new book of quilting designs. The border on the crib quilt came from a doodle.

You must think ahead when adding quilting that shows to crazy quilted sections so that you don't end up with double batting under the crazy quilting. Batting must be added separately, either before or during construction, to the areas that will be quilted. Several different ways to do this are detailed in the directions for projects with quilting that shows.

My enjoyment of hand quilting does not prevent an appreciation of the advantages of machine quilting. I think that children's quilts, especially, should be machine quilted so that they can be loved, washed often, and used, used, used. Save heirloom quilting for a wedding gift and make a shower gift that will be used everyday, rather than put away for special occasions.

A useful tool for machine quilting is the "walking" foot. It solves the problem that is caused with a standard presser foot, which moves the top fabric along slightly ahead of the bottom fabric. This is a condition aggrevated by adding batting between the two, and often results in a pleat being formed when attempting to stitch across a previously stitched line. A walking foot, in effect, walks across the fabric rather than pushing it. It is well worth owning if you plan to do much machine quilting (and also is invaluable for sewing on velvet, Ultra Suede and for use in matching plaids.)

The Strawberries & Dreams quilt is particularly easy to machine quilt and should be a good introduction to machine quilting for those who have not tried it. If you want to explore other approaches to machine quilting, I recommend the books on the subject in the bibliography.

Wherever your designs come from, and whether you work by hand or machine, let quilting that shows add a special touch to your crazy quilting.

Blanket Stitch —
  Blanket Stitch Variation
Closed Blanket Stitch —
  Open-and-Closed Blanket Stitch
Double Closed Blanket Stitch —
  Blanket Fans
Blanket Stitch Variation —
  Alternating Blanket Fans
Cretan Stitch
Closed Feather Stitch — Shisha Mirror
Chain Stitch — Zig Zag Chain Stitch
Simplified Wheat Stitch — Open Chain Stitch
Chain Wave with Detached Clusters —
  Chain Variation
Chain Medallion — Chain Motif

Compare this embroidered block with the same block before embroidery, shown on page 10.

Chapter Five

Stitchery

Crazy quilting has a special attraction for two groups. The first are those whose primary interest is hand work. They like the idea of combining patchwork with stitchery, but are initially uneasy about the sewing machine construction of the blank. Once they try contemporary crazy quilting, they appreciate that the sewing machine lets them get to their first love, embroidery, more quickly.

The second are those who are drawn to crazy quilting because they are comfortable with the sewing machine. They sometimes seem horrified by the prospect of doing hand embroidery. ("That takes a lot of time!") My first tactic was to convince them that it doesn't take that much time and, furthermore, it is easy and fun. I became aware that others were approaching it from another direction as I traveled around the country. People showed me projects made from my first book using machine embroidery, and several teachers told me they used the book as a resource in machine embroidery classes.

I still prefer hand embroidery — perhaps because it's how I relax after crazy quilting at the machine for hours — but the embroidery possibilities of the sewing machine are tremendous and I urge you to give it a try. If you haven't done it before, the instruction book for your sewing machine is the best place to start. There are listings in the bibliography for those who wish more information and the Strawberries & Dreams quilt for inspiration.

The amount of embroidery used should be determined by the piecing, the type of fabric used, the function of the project and the time you have available. On a completed blank, first embroider the curves. That gets the pins out of the way and gives you a chance to survey the blank to see where more embroidery is needed. When closing the curves, stitch through the entire blank to give those seams the same texture as the ones sewn on the machine. You are, in effect, quilting with embroidery. It is not necessary to stitch through the entire blank when embroidering on the machine sewn seams. If the fabric is very heavy or the blank has a Pellon backing, it is easier just to embroider through the fabric.

When my students realize that the curves must be closed by hand, their reaction is often alarm that they are "only" embroidered in place. If this is also your reaction, remember that Victorian crazy quilts are constructed entirely with embroidery. Deterioration is more often found in the fabric of these old quilts than in the embroidery.

What kind of thread should you use? Experiment with as many as you can find, taking into consideration the fabric, the look you want and how the project will be used. When I use embroidery floss, I use all six strands because I think it looks best with the texture of the crazy quilting. I use #5 perle cotton a great deal; it's especially nice for attaching shisha mirrors. The Victoriana quilt and the desk set are embroidered with a nylon velvet thread that gives an extra touch of luxury. Gold metallic thread was used with one strand of gold embroidery floss for one of the soft jewelry sets. It's more difficult to stitch with, but the effect is worth it.

There is no need to use a hoop when embroidering crazy quilting. The completed blank has enough firmness. Embroider with a darning needle. If you are used to stitching with an embroidery needle, you will feel you're using a dagger, but it makes it easier to pull the thread through the blank — easier on you and easier on the fabric. The velvet thread requires a special needle that will not cut the plush of the velvet.

STITCHERY

The stitches shown here are suggestions, a start for your personal collection or perhaps additions to your favorite stitches. I have not repeated any embroidery directions from my first book except to show the blanket stitch as the basis for some more variations. If you examine the stitches on the projects in this book, you will see some not included in this chapter. They can be found in my first book, and probably in most basic books on embroidery. Check the bibliography for further sources.

Don't judge your block until you have embroidered it. This advice is directed particularly at beginners, who often cannot picture the effect it will have and are discouraged that it doesn't look right. Stitchery has an impact on the finished piece. So does the absence of stitchery, as you can see from the Ice Ray and Crazy Amish quilts. The decision to work with or without embroidery should be based on the visual impact you are trying to achieve, not on tradition. Experiment with as much or as little embroidery as you like.

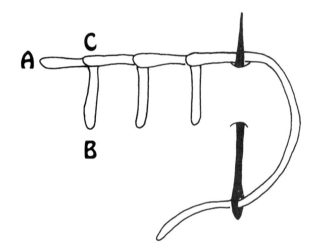

The **Blanket Stitch** is the basis for a wide range of variations. Bring the needle through at the line to be followed (A). Insert the needle at a right angle to the thread at the desired depth (B) and cross over the thread (C). Pull to form a loop.

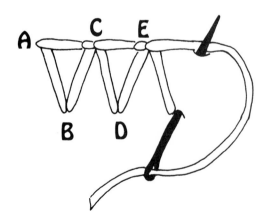

Closed Blanket Stitch. Bring the needle through at the line to be followed (A). Insert it at the depth desired below the line (B) and cross over the thread at the starting point (A). Insert the needle again at B, crossing over the thread at C. Continue in the same sequence, next working from D to C, and D to E.

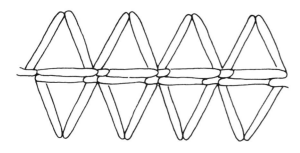

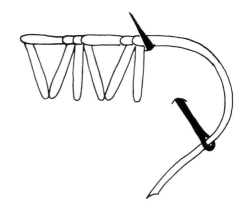

Double Closed Blanket Stitch. Work one row of the closed blanket stitch. Turn it upside down and work back, lining up the points.

A **Blanket Stitch Variation,** is alternating the basic stitch with the closed blanket stitch.

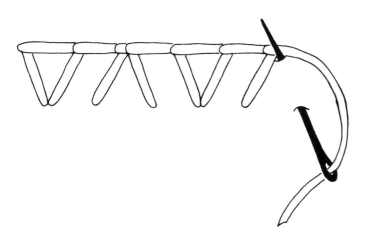

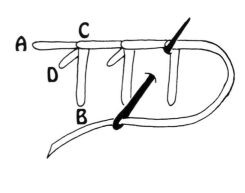

Open-and-Closed Blanket Stitch. Alternate the closed blanket stitch with diagonal stitches. Further variations along these lines can be achieved by working the units at differing depths.

Another **Blanket Stitch Variation** is formed by working the basic blanket stitch (A-B-C) and then inserting the needle at D, emerging at the angle at C.

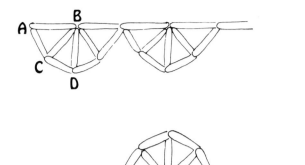

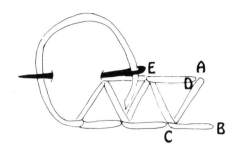

Blanket fans are another variation of the blanket stitch and can be done with any number of spokes. Bring the needle through at the line to be followed (A). Insert it half the desired width of the unit (B) and bring it out again at A. Insert the needle again at B, bring it out at C, crossing on top of the thread to form a loop. Reinsert the needle at B, bringing it out at D. Continue in this sequence until the fan is complete. Fans can be all worked in the same direction, or alternated.

Closed Feather Stitch. Bring the needle through at A and insert it at B. Come out at C over the thread, forming a loop. Insert the thread at D, coming out at E over the thread.

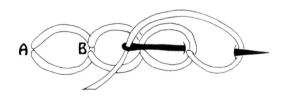

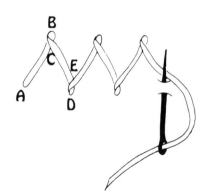

Chain Stitch. Bring the needle through at A. Circle the thread counterclockwise, holding it with the left thumb. Insert the needle at A, bringing it out at B to repeat the sequence. To end the chain, take a final small stitch over the last chain; see Detached Chain Stitch (p. 26) for detail.

Cretan Stitch. Bring the needle through at A. Take a stitch downward from B to C over the thread. Take the next stitch upward from D to E over the thread. Alternate upward and downward stitches, always pointing the needle in.

Shisha mirrors seem a natural embellishment for crazy quilting. They are little glass mirrors from India, usually irregular in shape. They are machine washable, although they are breakable if handled roughly. Ellen Mosbarger has allowed me to use directions that she has worked out for attaching them. The usual stitch for attaching the mirrors is the cretan stitch, but the blanket stitch is another possibility.

1. Thread a needle with 6-strand embroidery floss or perle cotton and knot the end. Hold the shisha on the cloth between your thumb and index finger. Come up from underneath with the thread just under the edge of the mirror. Go across the mirror and under on the opposite side (a-b). Come up again under the edge parallel to the first thread (c-d). Pull snugly.

2. Come up under the edge on the left side. As you cross the mirror take a "stitch" around each of the threads and go under on the opposite side (e-f). Come up again just a fraction from the previous thread and stitch around each thread (in the opposite direction) as you return (g-h).

3. Bring the needle up from underneath so that the thread comes out at the bottom edge of the mirror. Work the cretan stitch through the thread framework and at the edge of the mirror, one stitch taken upward and one taken downward.

4. Confusion sometimes arises about which side of the needle the thread goes on. If you remember that the tip of the needle must always pass over the working thread, you will be rewarded with the scroll design of the stitch.

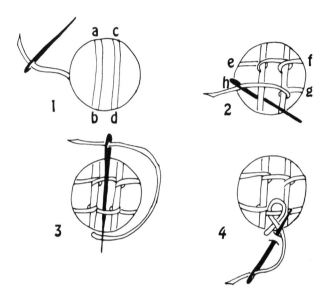

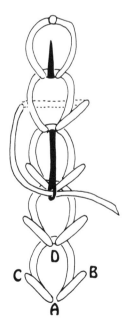

Simplified Wheat Stitch. Work a line of chain stitches. Starting again at the beginning of the chain, bring the needle through at A. Insert needle at B, emerging at C. Reinsert needle at A, emerging at D to repeat the sequence.

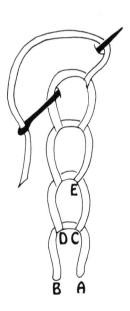

Open Chain Stitch. Bring the needle through at A. Circle the thread counterclockwise and hold it in place with your thumb. Insert the needle from B to C, over the loop. Repeat the sequence from D to E.

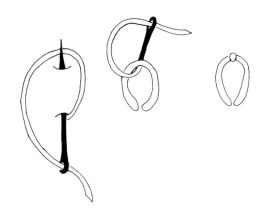 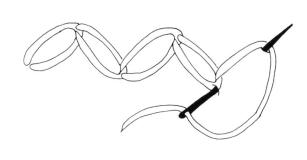

Detached Chain Stitch. The stitch is worked in individual units in the same manner as the chain stitch. Detached chains can be used to create designs and details, alone or in combination with other stitches.

Zig-Zag Chain Stitch. This is worked like the chain stitch, except that each stitch is taken at a right angle to the previous one and the needle pierces the thread of the previous chain to hold it in position.

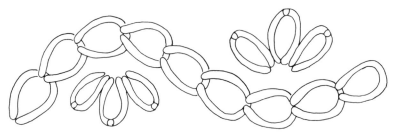

Chain Wave with Detached Clusters. An example of the designs that can be made by combining chain stitches.

Chain Variation. Work a line of chain stitches. Work two detached chains in the same side of every other chain.

Chain Medallion and Motif. Two examples of detached chain designs that can be worked to fit a specific area.

Chapter Six

Style Shows

Quilted clothing creates excitement among quilters and non quilters alike. A commercial pattern and a little crazy quilting can give individual style, even for those who have never thought of themselves as designers. Study the photographs of crazy quilted clothing on page 30. Look at the commercial pattern books with crazy quilting in mind to see where you can add a personal touch. You may want to carry designing in the cloth even farther and examine some of the books by Yvonne Porcella listed in the bibliography.

Once you have decided on the style of your garment, weight is an important factor to consider. Needlepunch or lightweight batting and a batiste weight backing are best for making the blanks to be used for clothing. If the quilted section is to be lined, you may want to try making the blank with paper or one of the removeable materials to cut down on bulk. When you are using heavy fabrics for the crazy quilting, you may wish to use no batting at all. The denim skirt and vest were pieced over a batiste base, with no batting, because of the weight of the denim.

Remember that the quilting will somewhat reduce the size of the blank and allow for this when picking your size. With a loosely fitted garment, you will be safe with your regular size. Fitted clothing that you intend to quilt completely, such as the denim vest, should be made on a blank a size larger than you normally wear. Adjust it to fit as the clothing is constructed. A fitted garment where only part of the pattern is quilted can be adjusted in the blank. Cut it about 1/4″ larger on all sides. After the crazy quilting and embroidery are finished, check it against the pattern piece and trim to fit, if necessary.

When constructing the blank, use the seam allowance indicated on the pattern, and trim the batting from the seam allowance before starting to quilt. If the crazy quilting will involve two or more pattern pieces, join the seams in the backing fabric before constructing the blank so the piecing will be uninterrupted by seams. If seams must be made in the crazy quilting, have them in the most inconspicuous place possible. The seams in the grey vest were joined across the shoulders in the backing piece, with the side seams joined when the quilting was completed and the garment was being constructed.

Shallow darts can be made in the backing fabric before the blank is constructed. This was done on the man's vest and caused no problems in the quilting or the fitting. If you must take deeper darts that would make the blank difficult to work on, take them after the crazy quilting is completed, but before you embroider. The embroidery can help disguise the dart.

Don't assume that you can wear quilted clothing only in cool weather. You can have a year-round wardrobe if you choose your style and fabrics carefully. The tunic and pants, for instance, are loose fitting, made of lightweight fabric, and quilted in such a way that they can be worn on the hottest day. The camisole dress was made suitable for summer wear by leaving out the batting and using a variety of weights and types of fabric to add the texture that usually is furnished by the batting.

Whether you crazy quilt an entire garment or add just a little trim, let your style show the year round.

Epilogue: Beyond Folk Art

Victorian crazy quilting is judged most often as folk art. Many who enjoy contemporary crazy quilting are first attracted to it by nostalgia, and essentially want to do a Victorian quilt more quickly. There is nothing wrong with this, but I believe that contemporary crazy quilting can add a new dimension to fiber art.

The last two quilts in the project section are first attempts to use this technique to design in cloth with the freedom artists have regardless of medium. These quilts provided an exciting challenge and I believe they establish the validity of the concept.

My main objective in working with a crazy quilt format is not to use a formula, but to continue experimentation and growth. The finest quilts being made today use contemporary perceptions to build on the creativity of previous generations. This book is written to give an additional tool to today's quiltmakers, not to chisel in stone a correct way to crazy quilt. Please use it to crazy quilt with a difference — YOUR difference.

Chapter Seven

The Projects

The following projects range from quick gift items to full size quilts. Since piecing becomes more complex on a larger blank, I recommend that beginners start with projects that use smaller blanks. This does not necessarily mean smaller projects. The Victoriana quilt, although queen size, uses a small blank that will not give a beginner any problems.

Yardages are given for the larger projects; measurements for the smaller ones will indicate amounts needed. Yardage requirements for the crazy quilting will vary depending on the number of fabrics used and the scale of the piecing. Linings or backing for the projects should prevent the stitchery on the back of the blank from showing through; darker solids or prints work best for this purpose.

Two different construction methods for the quilts are used, one for Strawberries & Dreams and Ice Ray, and another for Crazy Stars and Crazy Amish. The former involves less work while the latter gives a more traditional feel to the quilt. They are interchangeable; use the one you prefer. Victoriana is a special case and can most effectively be constructed as written.

Photographs of construction techniques used in several different projects are not repeated for each project, but are shown just once. You will be referred to the photo when the technique is repeated in a subsequent project. Unless otherwise stated, use 1/4" seam allowance in all construction.

Scotchgard fabric protector is useful in keeping the fabric from becoming soiled on projects that will receive a lot of handling, such as book covers, cosmetic bags and the like. Test a scrap of fabric before spraying and respray after washing.

Tunic and pants:
Shisha mirrors add a festive
note to this tunic and pants
outfit. Directions for attaching
the mirrors are given in the
Stitchery chapter. *Courtesy,
Folkwear, Inc. Photo by
Dave Johnson.*

Man's vest:
Ultra suede gives this vest a
special touch, whether worn with
jeans or with a dress suit. *Photo
by Kate Montgomery.*

Grey vest:
Quilting that shows complements crazy quilting to
give elegance to this vest. Quilting design from
NEEDLEWORK CLASSICS, by *Rebecca S. Cordello,
courtesy of Butterick Publishing, New York, NY.*

Quilter's Pocket

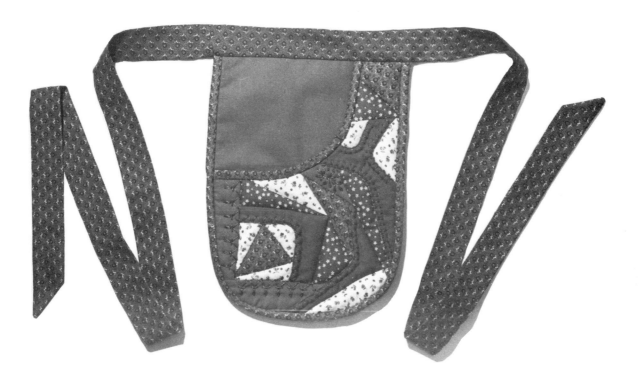

A quick project and a useful one — keep your quilting supplies at your fingertips!

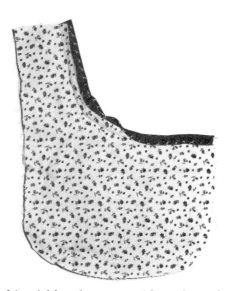

Construct blank of Pattern A (following page). Crazy quilt and embroider as desired. Pin the pocket front lining and the crazy quilted blank together, wrong sides facing. Press the 2″ bias in half down the center. Stitch the bias through all layers, with the raw edges of the bias lined up with the raw edges of the pocket.

Roll the bias fold to the wrong side and sew down by hand, just covering the machine stitching.

B

A

Label "B" (entire shape)

Label "A" (inside dotted line)

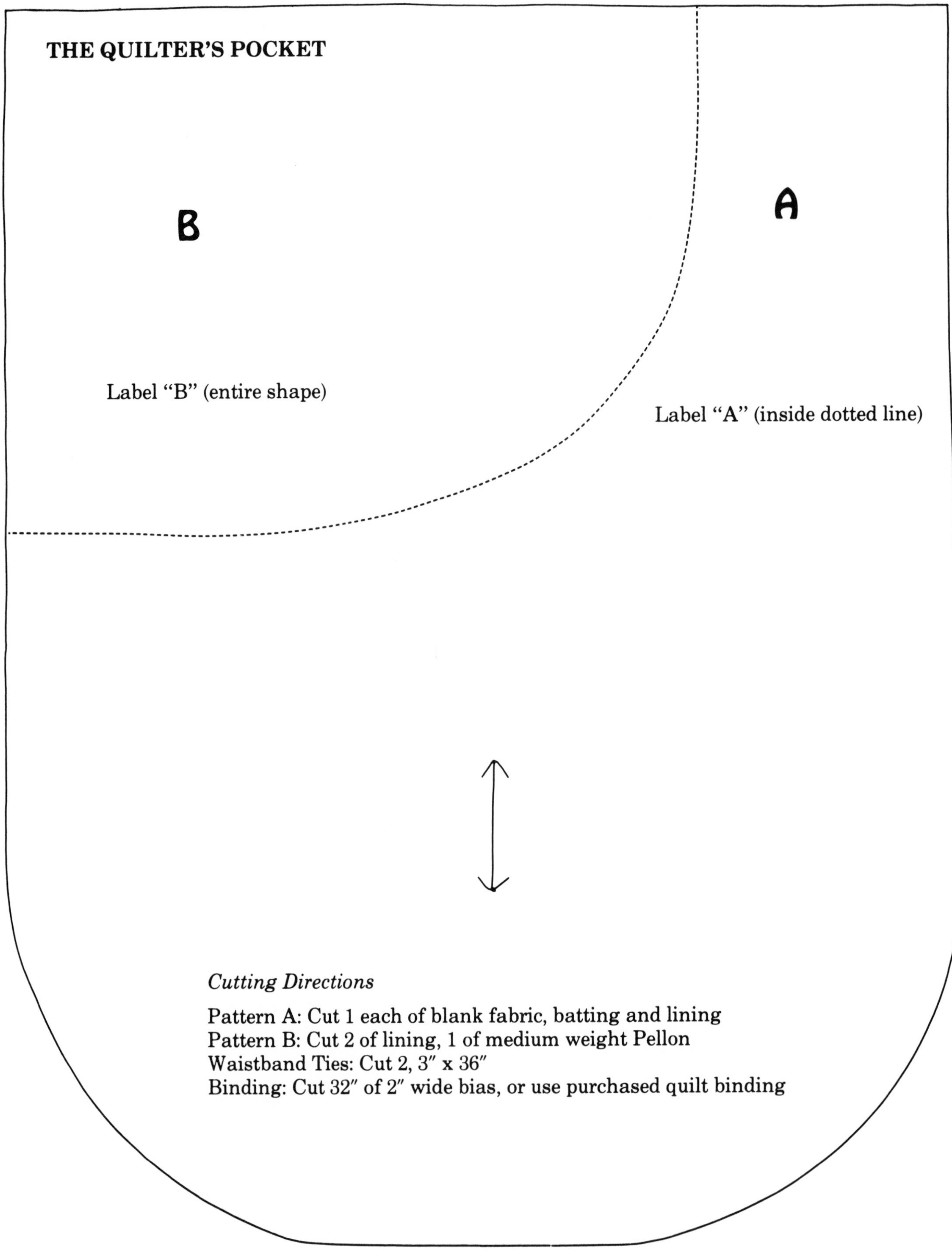

Cutting Directions

Pattern A: Cut 1 each of blank fabric, batting and lining
Pattern B: Cut 2 of lining, 1 of medium weight Pellon
Waistband Ties: Cut 2, 3″ x 36″
Binding: Cut 32″ of 2″ wide bias, or use purchased quilt binding

Pin the Pellon between the pocket back linings. Pin the pocket on top of the pocket back and stitch the bias around the edge. Turn to the back and close by hand.

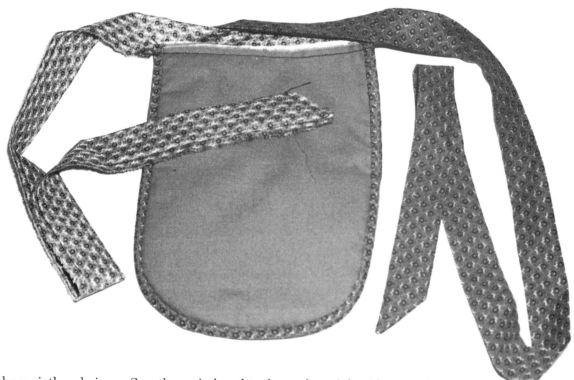

Join the waistband pieces. Sew the waistband to the pocket, right sides together, placing the seam of the waistband at the right edge of the pocket. Fold the waistband in half, right sides together, and pin along the ties. Cut an angle at each end of the ties. Sew the ties together. Turn right side out and close the waistband across the back of the pocket by hand.

Book Covers

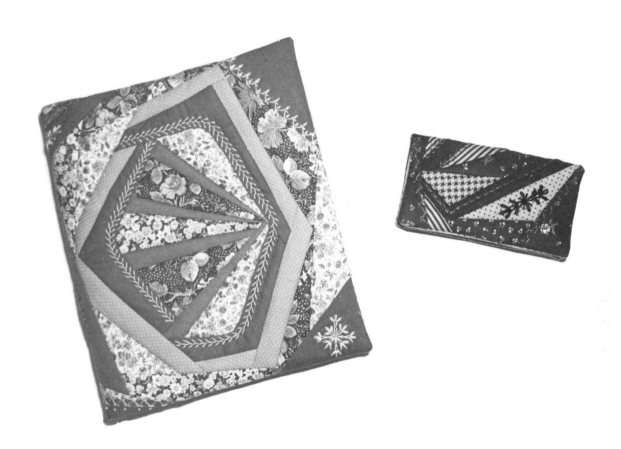

Give your books a special look, from checkbook to family album.

Cutting Directions

Checkbook Cover:

Cover — 7½″ x 8″. Cut 1 each of medium weight Pellon, batting and lining fabric.

Pockets — 6″ x 7″. Cut 2 of fabric.

Pocket interfacing — 3″ x 7″. Cut 2 of medium weight Pellon.

 To make other size book covers: Measure the book, adding 1″ to the height and 2″ to the distance around the book. Adjust the pocket height to match the cover, and about 1″ narrower than the cover.

Construct the blank using Pellon as a backing. Crazy quilt and embroider as desired. Prepare the pockets by pressing in half lengthwise and inserting the interfacing. Pin the pockets to both ends of the crazy quilted cover, with the folds at the center.

Pin the lining over the pockets, pulling taut. Fold one end back ¼. Sew around entire cover, but do not catch the folded edge of the lining in the stitching.

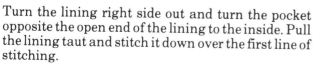

Turn the lining right side out and turn the pocket opposite the open end of the lining to the inside. Pull the lining taut and stitch it down over the first line of stitching.

Turn the other pocket to the inside. Fold the cover in half and press the fold.

Desk Set

Dress up your desk with this set. An added bonus: Turn the writing pad upside down, with the fabric side up, when you are marking fabric. The fabric on the writing pad will keep the fabric you are marking from moving.

Cutting Directions

Writing Pad:

Base — 16″ x 21″. Cut 2 of fabric, one for lining and one for the bottom.
Cut 1 each of medium weight Pellon, 40 mil plastic and blotter paper.

Pockets — 3½″ x 16″. Cut 2 each of batting, medium weight Pellon and lining.

Supplies needed:
Blotter, 15″ x 20″
40 mil plastic, 15″ x 20″

Note Pad Cover:

Cover — 6½″ x 14½″. Cut 1 each of medium weight Pellon, batting and lining.

Pocket — 6″ x 6½″. Cut one of medium weight Pellon. 6½″ x 12″. Cut one of fabric.

Supplies needed:
Note pad, 5½″ x 6″
40 mil plastic, 5½″ x 6″

Notes:

1. If you cannot find a blotter in the desired color, mat board is a good substitute. A wide selection of colors can be found in most stores carrying picture framing supplies.

2. If a different size note pad is used, adjust the size of the cover and the pocket.

3. The construction for the desk set is essentially the same as for the book covers, with variations in the pockets. Read the directions for constructing the book covers before starting this project.

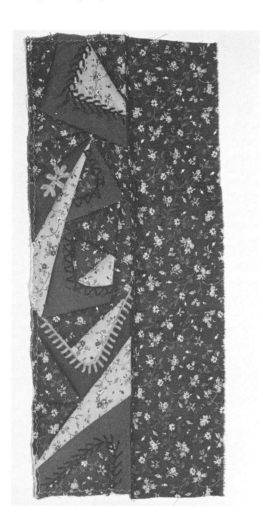 

Construct the blanks for the writing pad pockets using Pellon as the backing. Crazy quilt and embroider as desired. Sew the lining piece to the crazy quilted piece on one long edge, right sides together. Open right side out and edge stitch on the lining, ⅛″ from the seam. Fold the lining to the back and press the edge firmly.

Pin the Pellon under one piece of the base fabric. Pin the crazy quilted pockets on each end, right sides together. Add the lining and finish in the same manner as for the book cover. Insert the blotter with the plastic underneath for a firm writing surface.

Construct the blank for the note pad cover using Pellon as the backing. Crazy quilt and embroider as desired. Press the pocket fabric in half and insert Pellon inside. Pin the pocket to the top of the pad cover.

Pin the lining in place in the same manner as the book cover, folding the seam allowance back on the end with the pocket. Sew the lining and finish. Turn to the right side and insert the note pad into the pocket with the plastic underneath for a firm writing surface.

Clutch Bag and Cosmetic Bag

A matched set for yourself or for a special gift.

Cutting Directions

Clutch Bag:

Cut 1 each of heavy weight Pellon, batting and lining from Diagram A. Trim ½″ from the end of the lining.

Cosmetic Bag:

Cut 1 each of medium weight Pellon, batting and lining from Diagram B. Trim ¼″ from the end of the lining.
Button loop — 1″ x 4″. Cut 1.

Supplies Needed:

1″ piece of Velcro fastening tape for clutch bag, 1 button for cosmetic bag.

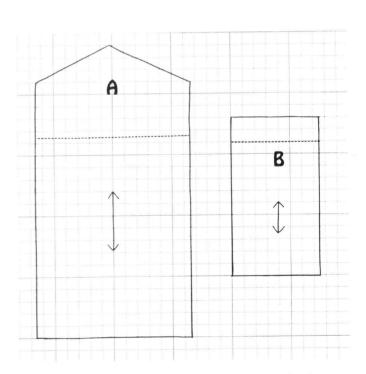

Pattern diagrams for clutch bag (A) and cosmetic bag (B). One square equals one inch. Fold on broken line for flap.

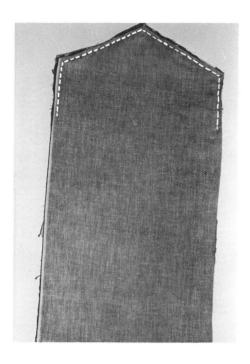

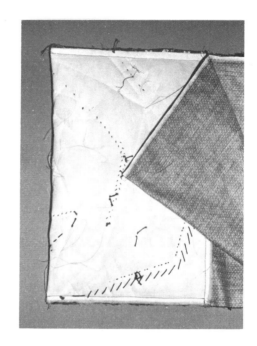

Construct the blank of Pellon and batting. Trim the batting from the seam allowance at each end of the blank before each starting to crazy quilt. Crazy quilt and embroider as desired. For the cosmetic bag, make a button loop and pin it to the right side of the center top. Lay the lining on the blank, right sides together. Match ends; the lining will be slightly smaller than the blank. Stitch across each end and down the side of the flap to the fold line.

Fold the unsewn sides of the bag to match and stitch together. Fold one side of the lining to match and stitch.

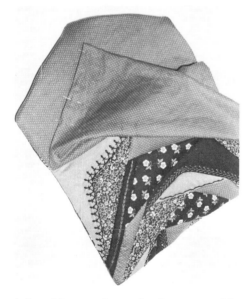

Turn right side out through the open side of the lining and stitch closed by hand or machine.

Finish the inside by stitching the lining to the blank backing with a chain stitch. This will prevent the lining from rolling over the edge. Be sure not to stitch through the crazy quilting. Sew a Velcro square in place on the clutch bag. Sew a button to the cosmetic bag.

Mirror

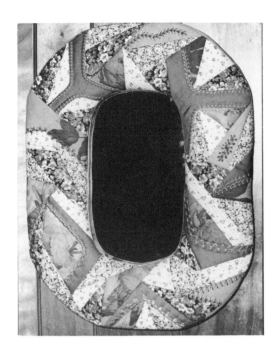

Mirror, mirror on the wall . . .

Construct the blank. Crazy quilt and embroider as desired. Lay the center facing over the opening right sides together and stitch. Cut out the center opening on the facing and clip around the curve. Sew bias around the outside, also clipping the curve.

Lay the crazy quilting on the plywood, right side up. Pull the center facing to the back of the plywood and staple in place, turning under the raw edges of the facing. Pad between the blank and the plywood with batting to the fullness desired; scraps of batting can be used. Pull the bias to the back of the plywood and staple, turning under the raw edges.

Fasten the mirror to the back with clamps, backing it with a piece of cardboard for protection. Attach a hanger.

MIRROR

Cutting Directions

Cut ¼″ plywood from the pattern as printed. Add 1″ to both the inside and outside edges of the pattern and cut 1 each of blank fabric and batting.

Center facing — 10″ x 14″. Cut 1 of fabric.

Bias — 2″ x 60″.

Supplies needed:
　　⅛″ mirror, 9″ x 13″

　　Cardboard, 9″ x 13″

　　Mirror clamps

　　Hanger bracket or wire

　　Staple gun

Pattern diagram one quarter full size. Fold paper both lengthwise and crosswise to make pattern.

Bread Cover

This is not only attractive, it also keeps your bread or rolls warm.

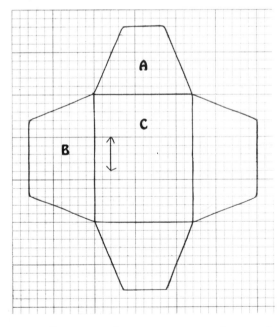

Pattern diagram. One square equals one inch. Patterns will be needed for the entire shape and for sections A, B and C.

Cutting Diagrams:

Cut 1 of whole diagram for inside.

A and B — Cut 2 each of blank fabric and batting for each pattern. Add ¼″ seam allowance on the longest edge.

C — Cut 1 each of batting and fabric for bottom.

Bias — 3 yards of 2″ wide bias, or use purchased quilt binding.

Note: This is designed for a 12″ x 15″ bread board. Adjust the measurements for another shaped board.

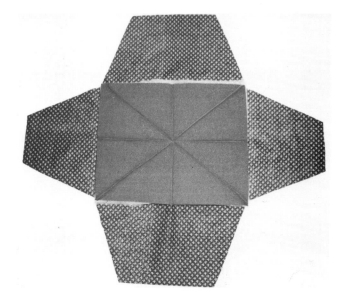

Construct the blanks of A and B, trimming the batting from the seam allowances on the longest side only. Crazy quilt and embroider as desired. Center piece C right side up on the wrong side of the lining. Put the batting between and stitch from corner to corner and side to side through the middle.

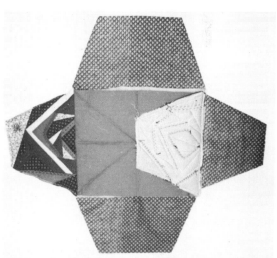

Sew the crazy quilted sides around piece C. Trim the batting under piece C from the seams. Open out the crazy quilted sides and pin to the inside fabric. Trim to match, if necessary.

Press the 2″ bias down the center and sew around the edge, finishing as was done in the quilters pocket (Project 1).

Basket Lids

Whether or not your favorite basket has a lid, make it special with a crazy quilted one.

For baskets without lids:

Make a pattern of the size needed to cover the opening, plus a ¾″ inch seam allowance. Cut one each of heavy weight Pellon, batting and lining.

Ties: Cut 4, 1″ x 5″ and 2, 1″ x 10″

For baskets with lids:

Make a pattern of the lid, plus ¾″ seam allowance. Cut one each of blank fabric and batting.

Supplies needed:

#100 cable cord and 1½″ bias, or purchased piping.

Note: If you don't wish to edge the lid with cording, cut a lining for the lid.

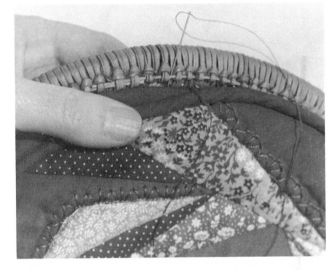

For a basket without a lid, construct the blank with a Pellon backing. Crazy quilt and embroider as desired. Check to see that the lid will fit; trim it if necessary. Fold the ties lengthwise and stitch the side and one end. Turn and press. Pin them to the top of the lid in the positions shown, with the shorter ties spaced at the back and the longer ones at the center front. Lay the lining on top, right sides together; and stitch, leaving an opening. Turn to the right side and close the seam. Press lightly on the wrong side. Tie the lid in place with the back ties.

For a basket with a lid, construct the blank with a fabric backing. After the blank is quilted, check the size, trimming it to fit if necessary. Cover cable cord with the bias, or use purchased piping and sew it around the lid. There is no need to line the quilting for a basket that has a lid if you use a corded edge. If you choose not to, finish the edge with a lining or baste under the seam allowance so that the edge will be smooth when you attach it to the lid. Sew the quilted top the lid, threading the needle through the edge of the basket.

Picnic Placemats

These placemats carry their own napkin and silverwear. They are made of denim, and don't have to be pampered; wrap them around the breakables and enjoy a picnic.

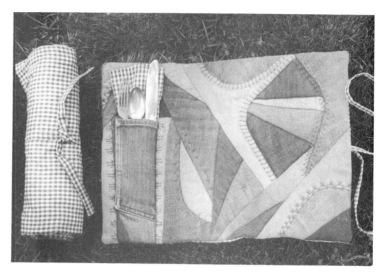

Cutting Directions:

For each placemat: 12½" x 17¼". Cut 1 each of blank fabric, batting and gingham lining.

Ties — 1½" x 12½". Cut 2.

Napkin — 14" x 16". Cut 1 of gingham.

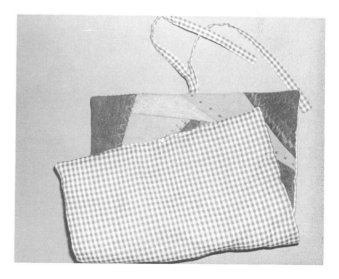

Construct the blank, trimming the batting from the seam allowance before starting to crazy quilt. Cut a jeans pocket in half, leaving some fabric around the pocket, and pin it on the left side of the blank. Crazy quilt with a variety of new and used denim, using the pocket as the first piece.

Fold the ties lengthwise and sew the sides and one end. Turn right side out and press. Pin the ties on top of the placemat at the end opposite the pocket. Lay the lining on top with right sides together and stitch, leaving an opening at the pocket end of the place mat. Turn right side out and close by hand. Hem the napkin and insert it in the pocket.

Pillow

Show off both your crazy quilting and your hand quilting on a pillow.

Cutting Directions

Pillow top — 12″ square. Cut 1 each of blank fabric and batting.

Pillow back — 18″ square. Cut 1 each of lining and back.

Border — 3½″ x 18½″. Cut 4 of fabric. Cut 2 pieces of batting 3″ x 18½″ and 2 pieces of batting 3″ x 12″.

Supplies needed:

1 invisible zipper. 12-14″ length.

16″ pillow form, or two 17″ squares of batting and batting scraps

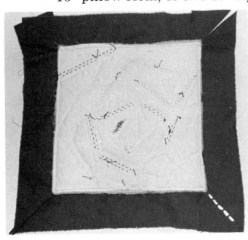

Construct the blank. Crazy quilt and embroider as desired. Check to see that the piece is square and trim, if necessary. To miter borders: 1. Sew a border strip to each edge, starting and stopping ¼″ from each end. 2. Press the corners back at right angles to form a miter (upper right corner). 3. Sew along the pressed lines (lower right corner). 4. Trim the seam to ¼″ and press open (lower left corner).

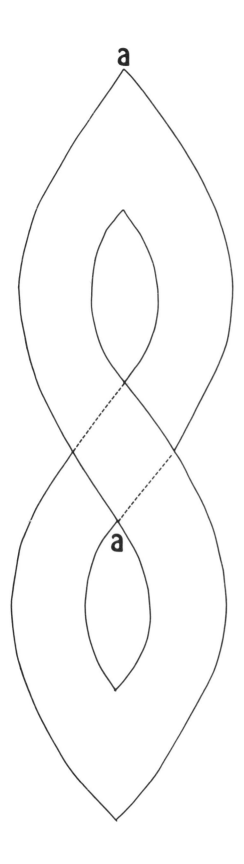

Mark the quilting design along the border. Add batting to the border, whipping it to the edge of the crazy quilting. Machine baste lining fabric to the pillow top, ¼" around the edge. Quilt the border. Sew an "invisible" zipper between the pillow top and the back, following the manufacturer's directions. (There is a special foot made for attaching these zippers, but a regular zipper foot also does a good job.)

Quilting design. Make a template of unit from a to a, and space around the border. Quilt along the solid lines for cable effect or on all lines.

Sew the pillow together and turn it right side out. Insert a pillow form, or make your own by sewing together two squares of batting, leaving an opening. Do **not** turn. Insert the form in the pillow, pushing the seam allowances firmly to the edges of the pillow. Fill the form with batting scraps and sew the opening closed. By inserting the pillow form into the pillow before stuffing, you can better gauge the amount of stuffing needed.

Christmas Tree Skirt

Put a star under your Christmas tree. This originally appeared in *Needlecraft for Today*.

Cutting Directions

Pattern A: Cut 4 each of red broadcloth and blank backing. Cut 8 of batting.

Pattern B: Cut 4 of blank backing.

Fabric Requirements

1¼ yards 45″ red broadcloth for solid sections.

2½ yards of red gingham for back.

1⅔ yards 36″ muslin (or 1¼ yards 45″) for blank backing.

Approximately ⅓ yard each of three assorted calicos and solids for the crazy quilting, plus the fabric left from cutting the back and solid sections.

Supplies Needed: 3 hook and eyes.

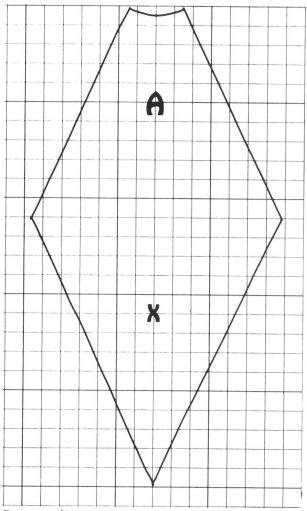

Construct 4 blanks from Pattern A using a ½″ seam allowance. Trim the batting from the seam allowance before starting to crazy quilt. Embroider as desired. Machine baste the batting to the red broadcloth with ½″ seam allowance and trim the batting from seam allowance. *Using no batting*, crazy quilt the 4 small stars on the backing. Turn under ¼″ seam allowance and applique to the broadcloth pieces with a blanket stitch.

Pattern diagram. One square equals one inch. Applique star at x.

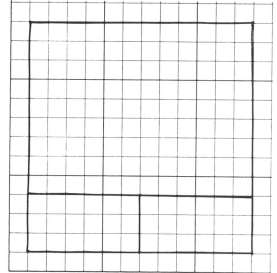

Piecing diagram for back. One square equals five inches.

Alternating solid and crazy quilted sections, sew the eight pieces together into a star, leaving one edge open. Follow the machine basting stitching as a guide when sewing. Using the piecing diagram, sew the gingham into a 60″ square. Lay the top on the gingham backing, right sides together, and use it to cut the backing. Sew completely around the skirt except for a 12″ opening along one side. Clip the center circle and the inner points. Turn right side out and close the opening by hand. Sew hooks and eyes at the top, middle and bottom of the open sides so that they just butt against each other.

CHRISTMAS TREE SKIRT

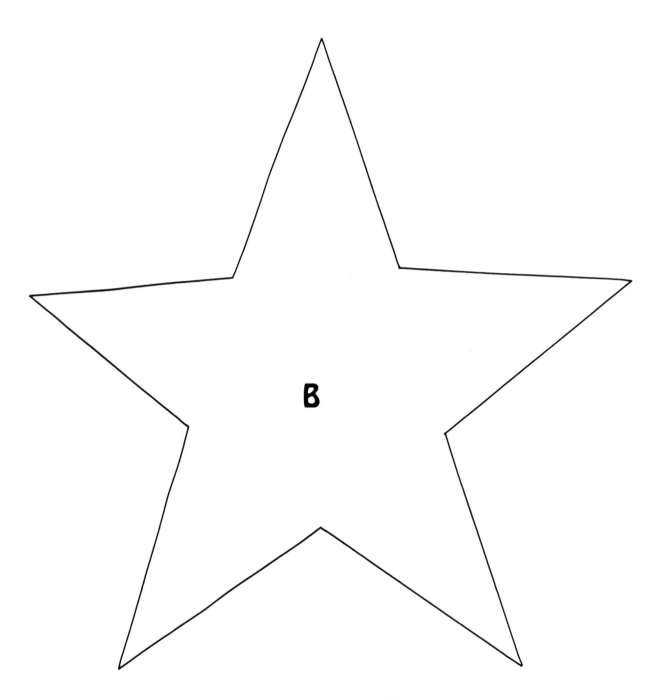

Full size pattern for star appliques.

Wall Piece

Cutting Directions

Center — 12″ square. Cut 1 each of blank fabric and batting.

Borders — 4½″ x 20½″. Cut 4 of fabric.

Back — 17½″ square. Cut 1 of fabric.

Padding — 20″ square. Cut 1 of batting.

Supplies Needed:

Four 17″ stretcher frame strips

Hanger bracket

Staple gun

Put your quilting on the wall. The stained glass effect is achieved by stitching around each piece in black thread with a chain stitch.

The top is constructed in the same manner as the pillow, except that no batting is added to the border and no lining is put on. Lay the top over a piece of batting and staple it to a stretcher frame.

Turn under a seam allowance on the backing and stitch it to the back, using a slip stitch. Put on a hanger bracket. Don't forget to sign your work!

Stool Cushion

Cutting Directions

For each cushion: Measure the stool, adding ¾" to all sides. Cut 1 each of blank fabric and batting.

Ties — 1½" x 11". Cut 8.

Back: Cut the length of the top and 3½" wider.

Supplies needed:

    3" Velcro fastening tape

    1" thick foam the size of the stool top

    Size #100 cable cord and 1½" bias; or purchased piping

You won't find stool cushions like these in your local stores!

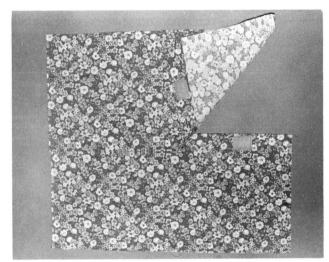

Construct the blank, using ½" seam allowance. Trim the batting from the seam allowance. Crazy quilt and embroider as desired. Check the completed blank against the stool. If it is more than ½" larger on all sides then you wish the finished cushion to be, trim off the excess. Cover the cable cord with 1½" wide bias, or use purchased piping, and sew it around the top. Fold the ties lengthwise and stitch the side and one end. Turn and press. Baste a pair of ties to each of the corners, putting each tie 1" tie from the corner.

Cut the back fabric in half lengthwise. Press under ¼" on one side of each piece and make a 1" hem. Sew three 1" pieces of Velcro evenly spaced on either side of the hemmed edges. Sew the back to the cushion top with the right sides together, using ½" seam allowance. Turn right side out and insert the foam cushion. Close the back with the Velcro fasteners.

Soft Jewelry

Have some fun with soft jewelry. One set is made with silk, gold thread and shisha mirrors; the other is of Ultra Suede. Construction is easy, so space has been used to give full size patterns rather than photographs.

Construction Directions

1. Construct the blanks, using ¼″ seam allowance. Trim the batting from the seam allowance. Crazy quilt and embroider as desired. Directions for applying shisha mirrors are given in Chapter V.

2. Sew cording to the edge, if desired. If the edges are corded, you will not need to understitch the lining.

3. Sew the lining to the top, right sides together, leaving an opening. (On the bracelets, leave the opening at one end.) Clip the curves. Turn right side out and sew the opening closed.

4. Sew hooks and eyes to the necklaces and to the bracelet in Set A. Sew the ends of the bracelet in Set B together to make a circle.

5. When the edges are not corded, stitch around the edge of the lining with a chain stitch as was done on the clutch bag.

Cutting Directions

Cut all edges with broken lines on the fold.

Set A: Necklace — Combine A-1 and A-2 at notches to make a pattern.
 Bracelet — Pattern C.

Set B: Necklace — Combine B-1 and B-2 at notches to make a pattern.
 Bracelet — 2″ x 10½″.

Cut each piece you are making with 1 each of blank backing, batting and lining.

Supplies needed:

 Hooks and eyes.
 Thin cable cord or purchased piping.

Note:

1. The bracelet in Set A is close fitting; the one in Set B is loose.
2. For firmer bracelets, use medium weight Pellon as the blank backing.
3. Instructions for applying the Shisha Mirrors are on p. 25.

A-1

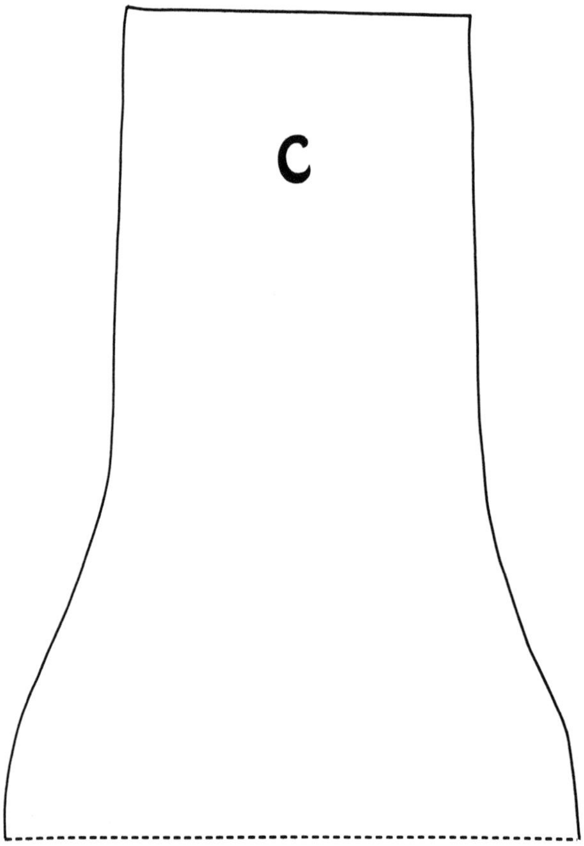

C

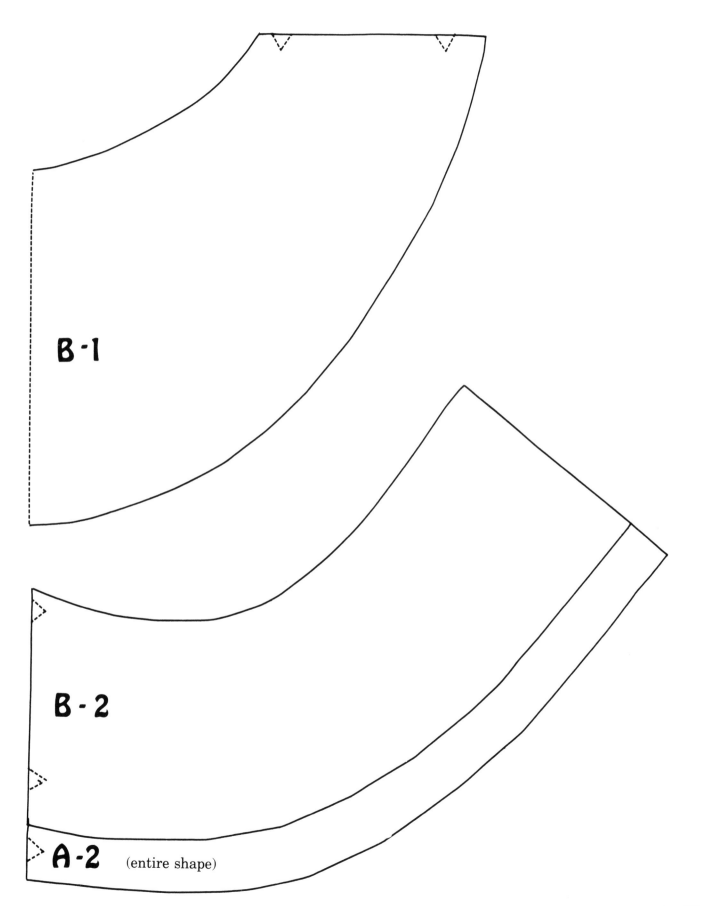

B-1

B-2

A-2 (entire shape)

Hostess Apron

Greet your guests in a crazy quilted hostess apron; it looks great over pants or a long skirt.

Cutting Directions

Patterns A and D — Cut 1 each of lightweight blank backing and batting.

Patterns B and C — Cut of apron fabric.

Lining — Cut 1 each of A-B and C-D of lining fabric.

Shoulder Straps — 5″ x 24″. Cut 2 of apron fabric.

Waistband — 3″ x 27″. Cut 2 of apron fabric.

Ties — 5″ x 31″. Cut 2 of apron fabric.

Fabric requirements:

Apron — 1½ yards 45″ fabric or 1⅞ yards 36″ fabric.

Lining — 1¼ yards 45″ fabric or 1½ yards 36″ fabric.

Supplies needed: 2 buttons

Note: ½″ seam allowances are used throughout.

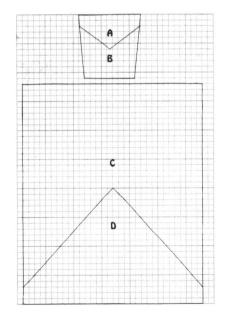

Pattern diagram. One square equals one inch. Add ½″ seam allowance to patterns for A, B, C, and D on the edges with broken lines.

2.

Sew A to B to form the bib. Sew C to D to form the skirt. Optional: Appliqué a band 1″ below the crazy quilting in the bib and 2″ above the crazy quilting in the skirt, using one of the fabrics from the crazy quilting and mitering the angle. In the apron shown, a border print was used in two different widths.

1.

Construct the blanks and trim the batting from the seam allowance. Crazy quilt and embroider as desired. On pieces B and D, stay stitch the angle by stitching on the seam line. Clip to the stitching.

4.

Center the bib between the two pieces of waistband, with the right sides of the waistband together. Sew the entire length of the waistband. Gather the skirt to 20″ and sew it to the top waistband, keeping the inside waistband out of the way. Sew the ties to each end of the waistband.

3.

Fold the shoulder straps lengthwise and sew along the side and across one end. Turn right side out and press. Taper the open end slightly and pin to the bib, ½″ from the side. Sew the lining to the bib, right sides together, around three sides, leaving the bottom open. Turn right side out and press. Line the skirt in the same manner.

5.

With the right sides together, sew the ties and the waistband closed to the skirt, cutting the ends of the ties to a right angle. Turn and press. Sew the inside waistband to the skirt by hand. (This step is shown in more detail on page 33). Make buttonholes in the waistband 1″ from the tie seam and sew the buttons in place at the ends of the shoulder straps.

Strawberries & Dreams Quilt

Give a new baby a bright welcome! Here's a quilt for sewing machine lovers; both the quilting and the embroidery are done on the machine.

Fabric Requirements All fabrics are 45″ wide.

Large strawberry print: 1 yard. For crazy quilting and quilt back.

Red pin dot: 1½ yards. For crazy quilting and quilt back border.

Green solid: 2 yards. For crazy quilt, front and back center strips and borders, and bias binding.

Muslin: 1½ yards. For blank backing.

Green calico and small strawberry print: ⅓ yard each. For crazy quilting.

Supplies needed: White machine embroidery thread.

Cutting Directions

Pattern A - Cut 4 each of blank backing, batting and large strawberry print.

Outside Border B - 6½″ x 37″. Cut 2 each of blank backing, batting and red pin dot.

Outside Border C - 6½″ x 49″. Cut 2 each of blank backing, batting and red pin dot.

Center Strip 1 - 4½″ x 19″. Cut 4 of green solid and 2 of batting.

Center Strip 2 - 4½″ x 37″. Cut 2 of green solid and 2 of batting.

Center Border 3 - 4½″ x 28″. Cut 4 of green solid and 1 of batting.

Center Border 4 - 4½″ x 37″. Cut 4 of green solid and 2 of batting.

2″ wide bias - Cut 6 yards of green solid.

Notes:

1. Cut borders, strips, backs and bias before starting to crazy quilt. Crazy quilt with the remaining fabric.

2. Borders and strips are cut slightly longer than necessary to allow for variances in the crazy quilting.

3. Fabrics are identified to make it easier to plan substitutions of colors or fabrics.

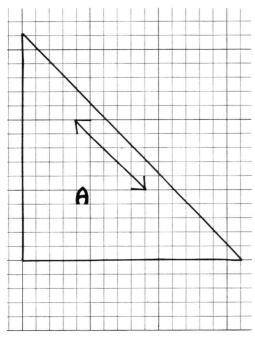

Pattern diagram for the center triangles. Add ¼" seam allowance to all edges. One square equals one inch.

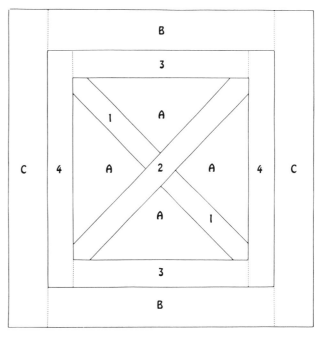

Quilt assembly chart. Letters denote crazy quilted sections; numbers indicate machine quilted sections. Graphed size: 47" square; actual size: 46" square.

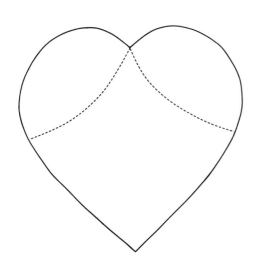

Template pattern for quilting. Make 1 template of the entire heart and 1 of the area below the broken line.

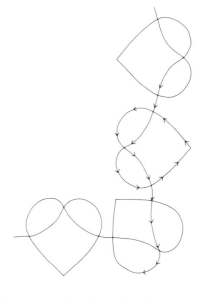

Quilting design for center border, showing the corner arrangement. This can be quilted in a continuous line by following the arrows.

STRAWBERRIES & DREAMS QUILT

Construct the blanks for the center triangles and the outside borders using ¼″ seam allowance. Trim the batting from the seam allowance on the triangles and on one side only of the border. The untrimmed side of the border will be the outside edge of the quilt. Crazy quilt all the blanks. To machine embroider, read the directions for your specific sewing machine. Back the blank with typing weight paper when machine embroidering to help it feed more smoothly. Remove the paper when you are finished.

Machine baste batting to half of the green strips and borders and trim the batting from the seam allowances. Pin a strawberry print triangle to a crazy quilt triangle, wrong sides together. Right sides together, pin a batted strip to the crazy quilt triangle and a plain strip to the strawberry print triangle. Following the machine basting line on the batted strip, sew all the layers together.

Open out the strips and pin the edges together. With the right sides together, pin a crazy quilted triangle to the top strip and the strawberry print triangle on the bottom. Stitch together, open out and pin the edges. You may need to trim the backing if the crazy quilting has reduced the size a little. Sew the remaining triangles to the second set of strips in the same manner.

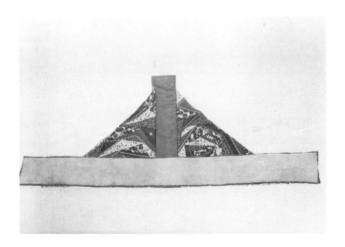

Center strips #2 on a pair of triangles and sew in the same way that strips #1 were sewn.

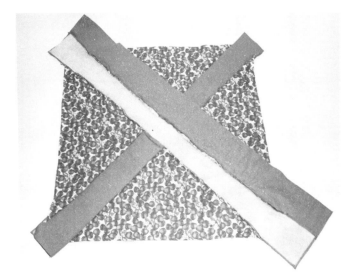

Sew the second pair of triangles only to the top strip, keeping the backing strip free and being sure to line up strips #1 to match.

Close the backing strip by hand. Square off the corners of the strips. Mark the quilting design by drawing around the heart template with a marking pen or pencil to make a unit of 4 hearts at the center. The arrow lines are right angles 1¼″ apart. Machine quilt, using a stitch length of 10-12 stitches to the inch. A walking foot is a great aid to smooth machine quilting, but if you don't have one, you'll not find it difficult to quilt this small strip. Start and stop by moving the stitch length to zero and taking 3 or 4 stitches in place to secure the thread.

Add the center borders #3 in the same manner that strips #1 were added. Trim off any extra length and add borders #4. Trim. Mark the quilting following the design on page 67, using the two templates made from the template pattern. It's easy to get the design even if you mark the corner hearts first, followed by the hearts in the center of each border, which will point the same direction as the corner hearts. Join the lines between the hearts freehand. Note that the angle of the lines in the corner hearts is slightly different.

Add the crazy quilted borders B and C, making sure the side of the border where the batting was not trimmed from the seam allowance is at the outside. Finish with a double bias binding, rounding the corners slightly. Detailed pictures of how to apply a double bias edge will be found in directions for the quilter's pocket. (Project 1).

Victoriana Quilt

The unusual combination of velveteen, eyelet and calico are used in this update of the Victorian crazy quilt. The back of the quilt repeats the design of the top in burgundy and navy cotton. Unfortunately, the colors are so close to the same values that this detail does not photograph well in black and white, but the effect in the cloth is worth the effort.

Fabric Requirements All fabrics are 45″ wide.

Burgundy velveteen: $6^2/_3$ yards. For quilt top and crazy quilting.

Burgundy cotton: $5\frac{3}{4}$ yards. For quilt back.

Navy cotton: 4 yards. For quilt back.

Muslin: 4 yards. For blank backing.

Three calico prints, white eyelet and broadcloth, navy velveteen: Total of 5 yards. For crazy quilting.

Cutting Directions

Pattern A - With a $\frac{3}{8}$″ seam allowance, cut 60 each of blank backing and batting.

  With a $\frac{1}{4}$″ seam allowance, cut 56 each of burgundy velveteen and burgundy cotton, and 60 of navy cotton.

Pattern B - With a $\frac{3}{8}$″ seam allowance, cut 4 each of blank backing and batting.

  With a $\frac{1}{4}$″ seam allowance, cut 4 of navy cotton.

Border 1 - $4\frac{1}{2}$″ x 74″. Cut 4 each of burgundy velveteen and burgundy cotton.

Border 2 - $4\frac{1}{2}$″ x 32″. Cut 4 each of burgundy velveteen and burgundy cotton.

$1\frac{1}{2}$″ wide bias - Cut 12 yards of burgundy velveteen.

Notes:

1. Velveteen makes this a lush quilt, but be aware that is also makes it a heavy quilt. This quilt weighs close to ten pounds.

2. Mark the nap direction on the velveteen when you are cutting it by pinning an arrow on each piece. Be sure all the arrows point the same direction when the quilt is being constructed.

3. Zig-zag the edges of the velveteen to prevent excessive raveling.

4. Cut the borders first, then cut the triangles and the bias. Use the remaining velveteen in the crazy quilting.

5. The blanks are cut larger to allow for some reduction caused by the quilting. The borders are cut slightly longer than necessary.

6. When crazy quilting with eyelet, back it with white broadcloth and sew and cut it as if it were one piece of fabric.

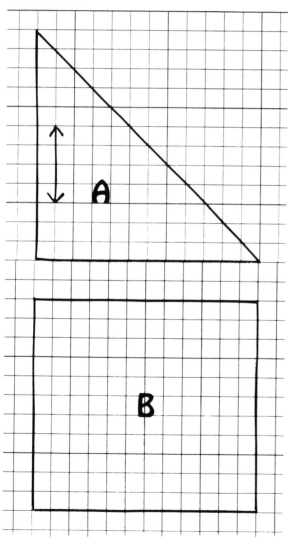

Pattern diagrams. One square equals one inch. The diagrams do not include the seam allowance; see the cutting directions before making templates.

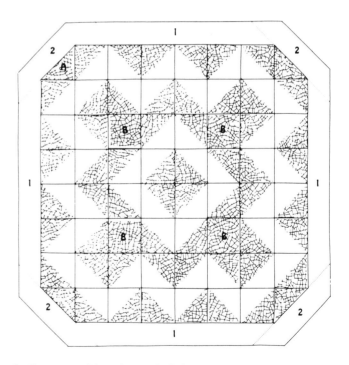

Quilt assembly chart. Solid areas are velveteen. Except four 4 squares (B), the quilt is composed of triangles (A). Graphed size: 104″ square; actual size: 100″ square.

VICTORIANA QUILT

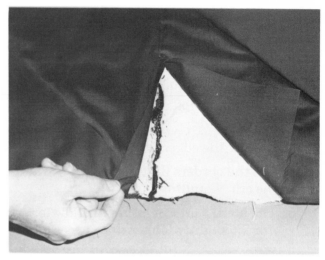

Detail showing construction of triangles into squares with the backing attached.

Detail showing squares joined into rows.

Construction Directions

1. Machine baste batting to the velveteen triangles and borders, using a ¼″ seam allowance. Trim the batting from the seam allowance on the triangles and one side of the borders. The untrimmed side will be the outside edge of the quilt.

2. Construct the blanks, using a ⅜″ seam allowance. Trim the batting from the seam allowance. Crazy quilt and embroider as desired. Measure the crazy quilted blocks against the corresponding backing pieces and trim them to the same size, if necessary.

3. Join the crazy quilted triangles to the velveteen triangles as follows:

    a. Lay the crazy quilt and the solid triangles together, with the right sides facing.

    b. Lay the backing triangles on top, with the right sides together. The wrong side of the navy triangle should be against the wrong side of the crazy quilt triangle.

    c. Stitch through all the layers, leaving 1″ unsewn at each end.

    d. Sew the fronts to each other at both ends. Then sew the backs to each other at both ends.

4. Open out the triangles to form a square. Following the assembly chart, join the squares into rows. Sew the fronts together by machine and press the seams open. (Use a light touch to avoid flattening the batting.) Sew the backs together by hand. It is a good idea to catch the seam allowances of the front with the thread as you join the backs except for the last inch at either end. The backs and fronts must be free of each other at the ends so the backs can be pulled out of the way when the fronts are joined into rows.

5. When the rows have been joined, add the borders in the same way they were added in the Strawberries & Dreams quilt. Put the longest ones on first and finish with the short pieces across the corners. Trim, if necessary. Be sure the side of the border with the batting in the seam allowance is on the outside edge of the quilt.

6. Finish the edge with the velveteen bias. Do not double fold the bias on this quilt because of the bulk of the velveteen.

Crazy Stars Quilt

Crazy quilted "stars" combine with hand quilted stars in a simple medallion quilt.

Fabric Requirements

All fabrics are 45″ wide.

Navy: 9¾ yards. For front and back borders, back of crazy quilted blocks, bias binding and crazy quilting.

Light rust: 3½ yards. For quilted squares, middle borders and crazy quilting.

Rust print: 3½ yards. For backs of quilted squares and middle borders.

Muslin: 1½ yards. For blank backing.

Fabric for crazy quilting: Total of 2 yards.

CRAZY STARS QUILT

Cutting Directions

12½″ square: Cut 12 of navy, and 7 each of light rust, rust print and batting.

13″ square. Cut 12 each of blank backing and batting.

Inner Borders: #1 - 4½″ x 60½″. #2 — 4½″ x 44½″.

 Cut 4 each of navy and 2 each of batting.

Middle Borders: #3 — 12½″ x 68½″. #4 — 12½″ x 44½″.

 Cut 2 each of light rust, rust print and batting.

Outside Borders: #5 — 6½″ x 92½″. #6 — 6½″ x 80½″.

 Cut 4 each of navy and 2 each of batting.

2″ bias — Cut 11 yards of navy.

Note:

1. The blank is cut larger to allow for reduction caused by the quilting. After crazy quilting and embroidering, measure the blocks and trim to 12½″ if necessary.

2. This quilt is made with a variation of the "quilt as you go" technique. The sections are added one at a time and then quilted before the next is added, rather than the other way around. Try it; it works.

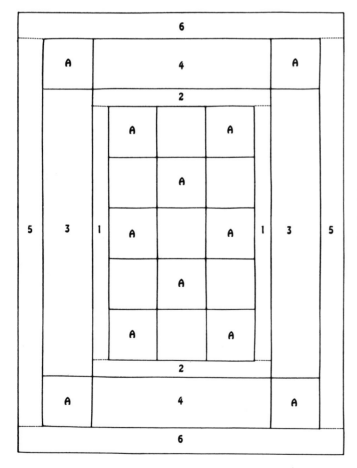

Quilt assembly chart. A indicates the crazy quilted blocks; the unmarked squares are hand quilted. The various borders are added in the number sequence. Size: 80″ x 108″.

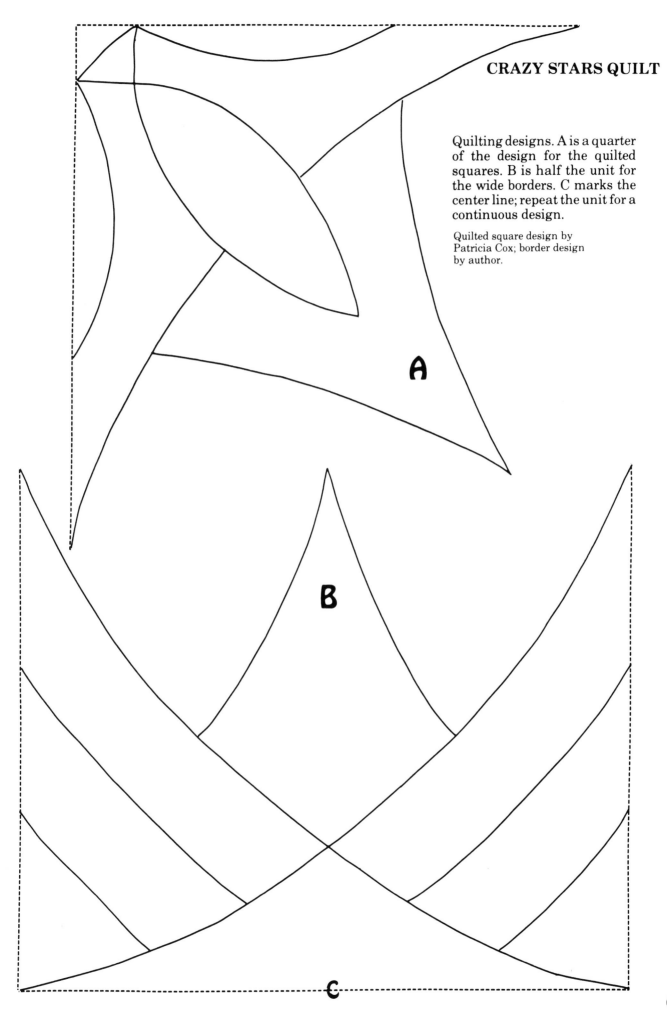

CRAZY STARS QUILT

Quilting designs. A is a quarter of the design for the quilted squares. B is half the unit for the wide borders. C marks the center line; repeat the unit for a continuous design.

Quilted square design by Patricia Cox; border design by author.

A

B

C

CRAZY STARS QUILT

Construct the blanks, leaving the batting in the seam allowances. Crazy quilt and embroider as desired. Baste a navy back to a crazy quilt block, wrong sides together. Mark the quilting designs in the light rust squares. Sew a light rust square to the crazy quilt block and a rust print back to the navy back.

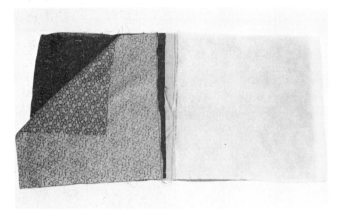

Whip a batting square to the edge of the crazy quilt square.

Baste the light rust square and hand quilt. Add the next crazy quilt square in the same way. sewing the tops and then the backs. Trim the batting if necessary to make it lay flat and whip it to the edge of of the crazy quilted block. Baste the block together. Construct the next 4 rows in the same manner.

Sew the front of a completed row to the front of the next row, pinning the backs out of the way.

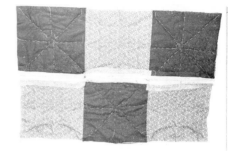

Trim the batting so it will lie flat and whip it to the edge of the crazy quilted squares. Work on a flat surface for best results.

Close the backs by hand, matching the corners.

Add borders #1 and #2 to the completed center section, sewing the tops and the backs together in the same way the rows were constructed. Mark the border quilting with diagonal lines going in opposite directions from the center. Lines marked 1¾″ apart should come out even at the corners (with any kind of luck!). Whip the border batting in place and baste the border down the middle.

Mark the quilting design on the middle borders. Sew borders #3 to the sides of the quilt as the other borders were added. Add batting under the border sections.

Baste securely and hand quilt the side border sections.

Sew the crazy quilted blocks to both ends of border #4. Measuring carefully so that the back will match, sew the crazy quilt backs to the border backs. Join to the top and back of the quilt in the same manner as the other borders were added. Whip the batting in place, baste and quilt.

Add borders #5 and #6, whip in the batting, baste and quilt in the same design as the inside borders. Finish with a double bias binding, rounding the corners slightly. Detailed pictures for the bias finishing will be found in the directions for the quilter's pocket (Project 1).

Ice Ray Quilt

Ice Ray will warm you as a lap quilt, or will look great on the wall.

Fabric Requirements All fabrics are 45″ wide.

Royal blue: 3 yards. For the back of the crazy quilt bars, front and back of the borders, and bias binding.

Orange: 1½ yards. For front and back of the bars.

Light blue, light orange and yellow: ⅓ yard each for crazy quilting.

Batiste or Stitch-n-Tear: 1½ yards. For blank backing. See note.

Cutting Directions

Bars and Border #1: 8½″ × 48½″. Cut 4 of orange, 3 of blank backing and 7 each of royal blue and batting.

Border #2: 8½″ x 56½″. Cut 4 of royal blue and 2 of batting.

2″ bias — cut 7 yards of royal blue.

Note: The crazy quilting in this quilt is double quilted — machine quilted in the piecing and then hand quilted in the seams as the quilt is constructed. The blank backing is made from a removeable material to make the hand quilting easier, but it can be made of a lightweight fabric if desired. Paper can also be used.

Quilt assembly chart. Size: 56" x 64".

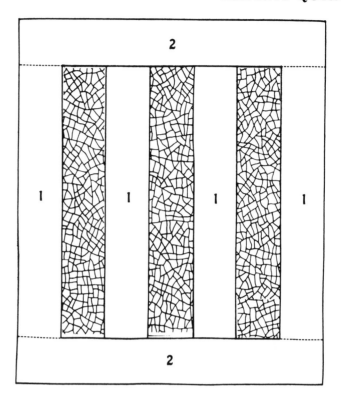

Construction Directions

1. Construct the blanks from batiste or Stitch-n-Tear, using a ¼" seam allowance. Trim the batting from the seam allowance. Crazy quilt as desired. If you have used Stitch-n-Tear, remove it after crazy quilting; do not zig-zag the edges of your blank until it has been removed. Slip stitch the curved seams.

2. Mark the quilting designs on the orange bars and on the borders. Machine baste batting to them, using ¼" seam allowance. Trim the batting from the seam allowance.

3. Baste a royal blue bar to the back of the crazy quilting, wrong sides together. Hand quilt with blue thread in the seams of the crazy quilting.

4. Lay an orange bar with the batting attached right side down on the crazy quilted bar. Lay the backing on the bottom, right sides together, and sew through all the layers, following the machine basting stitching. This technique is illustrated in the Strawberries & Dreams quilt.

5. Open the orange bar, baste and hand quilt with orange thread. Add the other bars and borders in the same way, quilting each one before the next is added.

6. Finish with a double bias binding, rounding the corners slightly. Detailed directions for the bias finish will be found in the directions for the quilter's pocket (Project 1).

Quilt design for the corners. The bar and border quilting design was adapted from a design for Chinese latticework from *CHINESE LATTICE DESIGNS* by Daniel Sheets Dye (Dover Publications, Inc., 1974). It is not reproduced here because it will be easy for you to duplicate the effect with random lines, ¼″ apart.

Crazy Amish Quilt

Inspired by the colors and set of an Amish quilt,
Crazy Amish combines traditional quilting designs
with free form crazy quilting.

The construction method results in a quilt with an
interesting back.

CRAZY AMISH QUILT

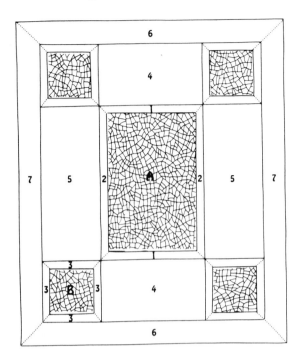

Quilt assembly chart. Size: 72″ x 84″.

Fabric Requirements All fabrics are 45″ wide.

Black: 4½ yards. For front and back outside borders, crazy quilting and bias binding.

Plum: 4 yards. For front and back middle borders and craazy quilting.

Grey: 2½ yards. For inside borders, back of crazy quilting and crazy quilting.

Burgundy and rose: ⅓ yard each for crazy quilting.

Batiste or Stitch-n-Tear: 1½ yards. For blank backing.

Cutting Directions

Blank A: 25″ x 37″. Cut one of blank backing and batting.

Blank B: 13″ square. Cut 4 each of blank backing and batting.

Inside borders.

    #1 - 2½″ x 28½″. Cut two each of grey and batting.

    #2 - 2½″ x 40½″. Cut two each of grey and batting.

    #3 - 2½″ x 16½″. Cut 16 each of grey and batting.

Middle borders.

    #4 - 16½″ x 28½″. Cut 4 of plum and 2 of batting.

    #5 - 16½″ x 40½″. Cut 4 of plum and 2 of batting.

Outside borders.

    #6 - 6½″ x 72½″. Cut 4 of black and 2 of batting.

    #7 - 6½″ x 84½″. Cut 4 of black and 2 of batting.

Crazy quilt backs.

    Cut 1 28½″ x 40½″ of grey.

    Cut 4 16½″ square of grey.

2″ bias: Cut 9 yards of black.

Full size quilting design for the inner borders, showing the corner detail. For the squares, repeat at the broken line. The rectangular border will extend beyond that point, but it should come out even. To be sure it does, start marking at the corners and adjust in the center if necessary.

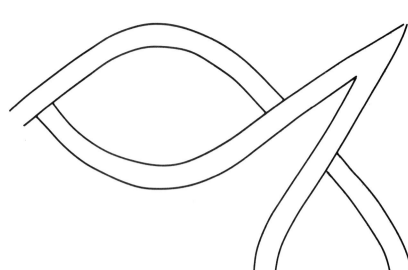

Notes:

1. The blanks are cut larger to allow for reduction caused by the quilting. After crazy quilting, measure the blocks and trim the center to 24½″ x 36½″ and the corners to a 12½″ square, if necessary.

2. This quilt is constructed essentially the same way as the Crazy Stars quilt (Project 17). Refer to the photographs for that quilt if a direction is not clear to you.

3. Like the Ice Ray quilt (Project 18), the crazy quilting is double quilted. The blank backing is made from a removeable material to make the hand quilting easier. Paper or a lightweight fabric can also be used.

4. Cut the border, backs and bias first. Use the remaining fabric for crazy quilting.

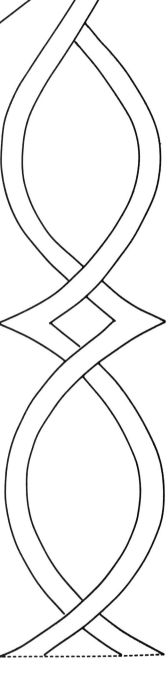

Detail of a blank constructed with Stitch-n-Tear, partially removed.

CRAZY AMISH QUILT

Construction Directions

1. Construct the blanks. It is not necessary to trim the batting from the seam allowance. Crazy quilt as desired. If you have used Stitch-n-Tear, remove it after crazy quilting; do not zig-zag the edges of your blank until it has been removed. Slip stitch the curved seams.

2. Add the grey borders to the crazy quilted sections, mitering the corners as shown in the directions for the pillow (Protect 10). Mark the quilting design on the borders. Add the batting to the borders, whipping it to the edge of the crazy quilting.

3. Baste the back to the center section, wrong sides together. Hand quilt in the seams of the crazy quilting and on the border design.

4. Mark the quilting design on the middle borders. Sew side borders #5 to the center section the way it was done on the Crazy Stars Quilt, sewing the top border to the top and the back border to the back. Whip the batting in place, baste and hand quilt. *Do not quilt the last inch* at the outside edges until the next borders have been added.

5. Add the crazy quilted squares to either end of middle border #4. Add the back for the crazy quilted squares to the back of middle border #4 the way it was done on the Crazy Stars quilt. Sew the borders to the quilt, whip batting in place, baste and quilt to within an inch of the edges.

6. Add the outside borders in the same way, mitering the corners. Mark the quilting, whip the batting in place, baste and quilt.

7. Finish with a double bias binding. Detailed directions for the bias finish will be found in the directions for the quilter's pocket (Project 1).

Quilting design for the wide border. To aid in reproducing the scale, the background lines are ¾″ apart. Leave off the outside feathers for border#4.

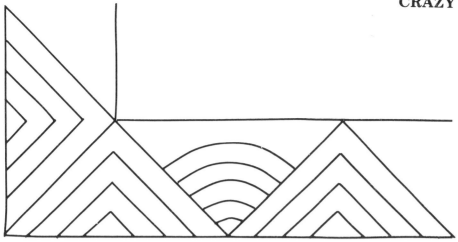

Full size outside border unit and corner detail. Repeat at the broken lines.

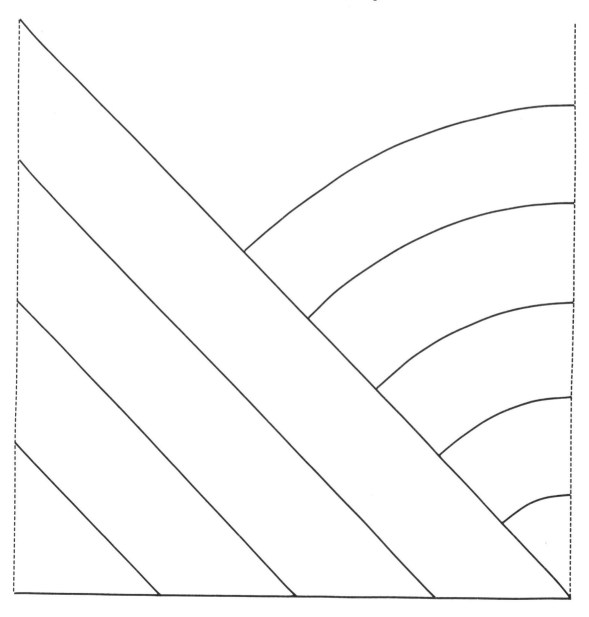

Bibliography

Clothing
Porcella, Yvonne. Five Ethnic Patterns, 1977. Self published.
_____Plus Five, 1978. Self published.
_____Pieced Clothing, 1980. Self published.

Machine Quilting
Fanning, Robbie and Tony. The Complete Book of Machine Quilting. Chilton, 1980.
Johannah, Barbara. Continuous Curve Quilting. Pride of the Forest, 1980.

Quilt Design Sources
Cordello, Rebecca. Needlework Classics. Butterick Publishing, 1976.
Cox, Patricia. Every Stitch Counts. 1981. Self published.
Dye, Daniel Sheets. Chinese Lattice Designs. Dover Publications, 1974.

Stitchery
Bond, Dorothy. Crazy Quilt Stitches, 1981. Self published.
Enthoven, Jacqueline. Stitches With Variations. Sunset Designs, 1976.
Fanning, Robbie. Decorative Machine Stitchery. Butterick Publishing, 1976.

Index

Italics indicate illustrations

ABOUT THE AUTHOR

Dixie Haywood made her first quilt in 1954, started her second in 1969 and has been quilting non-stop since. She has been teaching all forms of quiltmaking since 1974 and is a National Quilt Association Certified Teacher. Her designs and articles have appeared in many national publications and her work has won several awards.

As a result of teaching and custom work, she developed the technique of contemporary crazy quilting that was introduced in her first book. This new book is the result of four more years of experimentation with the technique.

A native of Washington State, Dixie lived all over the United States until her husband, Bob, retired from the Air Force. She currently lives in Pensacola, Florida.